I Love a Mystery

by
Bob Rybak

illustrated by Susan Kropa

Cover by Ted Warren

ISBN No. 0-86653-655-8

Printing No. 98765432

Good Apple
1204 Buchanan St., Box 299
Carthage, IL 62321-0299

SIMON & SCHUSTER *A Paramount Communications Company*

Dedication

This book is dedicated to my wife Sharon, my daughter Sarah and my son Paul for their ability to make me realize what is important in life and most of all for helping me keep my sense of humor.

Table of Contents

Literature-Based Reading–A New Idea?

At an International Reading Association conference I met a teacher from British Columbia, Canada. This was my first IRA conference; it was her eighteenth. She said something that sounded a little cynical at first and perhaps a bit jaded, but it contained a good deal of truth. "Honey," she said flatly, "I've been coming to these conferences for eighteen years and let me tell you something. There are no new ideas."

She wasn't saying that there are no *good* ideas, just that there are no *new* ideas. That's how I feel about literature-based reading. It certainly isn't new. The idea of teaching children the enjoyment of and the skills of reading using books is certainly not a revolutionary idea. We've been doing it ever since students were taught using the Bible. In education we tend to recycle our teaching ideas and theories. We update them; we change the jargon; we claim that they are new. Many times they aren't. But that doesn't mean they aren't effective.

Literature-based reading provides a tremendous reading experience for students. For many it will be the first time they ever finished a book from cover to cover that didn't have pictures on every page. It stretches their vocabularies and introduces them to verbal expressions common to our language. It weaves intricate plot patterns that they can follow and appreciate and thus builds comprehension. It provides three-dimensional characters to whom students can relate. Most of all, it fosters a love for reading. Students in my classes have gone on to read other books by the same author or other books of the same literary form all on their own. I have also seen them independently talking about books they've read and sharing them. In the intermediate grades that should be our primary task, to get students reading independently and making it their choice of something to do.

With literature-based reading the students read the stories as the authors wrote them, unedited and unabridged, in their full length and form. There are no workbook pages with unrelated skill lessons, no busy work. The stories are not cut down to fit into a large hardbound reader. The richness of the author's original wording is left in the text, and all the twists and turns of the plot remain intact. The students get the full benefit of the author's ability.

In school systems all over the United States, however, teachers are expected to do more than just expose students to good literature. As teachers, they are expected to meet certain objectives related to reading. These objectives involve promoting vocabulary development in students, developing reading skills such as sequencing, identifying main ideas, discerning between fact and opinion, verifying character development, etc. Basal readers have always provided support materials for those lessons, but if a teacher chooses to have students read a full piece of literature in its entirety, those support materials may be missing.

The big question with literature-based reading has always been, "Where do we get the materials we need to teach the skills and vocabulary that's expected of us?" For teachers using a literature-based approach, the job of bridging the gap between the literature and reading skills rests squarely on their shoulders since no teacher's guides are provided when a book is selected to use in a classroom. That could mean hours and hours of time relating the story to the school system's reading objectives and still more time creating original materials that students can use. This can make the use of literature-based reading more than any teacher bargained for. That's a legitimate complaint and one this book seeks to remedy.

Whole Class Grouping and the Teacher

Have you ever wanted to conduct reading class like science or social studies and have everyone reading and doing the same thing? What stops you? Usually it is because you've traditionally felt obligated to group students according to ability (usually three levels) so that each student is reading at his/her level.

What would it be like, though, to have everyone read the same book together? Would you miss meeting the needs of more able or less able students? Would reading class slow down to accommodate students who are less proficient? Would reading instruction become less effective? Simply put, no. Organizing reading instruction by having all class members reading the same book together holds distinct advantages for both the student and teacher.

For the teacher the first advantage is obvious. It reduces planning time. Teaching reading to three distinct groups is like juggling three balls. It requires total concentration on all three balls at all times. With all that effort put into keeping the balls going, there is little time to concentrate on anything else . . . like the students. Think about it. While you are conducting a reading lesson with a group of five to twelve students, you have to have effectively planned how the other fifteen to twenty-five students are going to be meaningfully engaged in education. That increases the necessary planning time and ultimately the amount of time grading papers (from the "meaningful" seatwork the students do while you are conducting a reading group).

Can a teacher better utilize her time? With a whole class reading format she can. One book, one class. Lessons are not repeated from one reading group to another. Instead everyone works together on the same skill or lesson. That's going to allow more time for you to circulate among students and provide instruction on individual student needs.

What about students who do need more or less instruction than the average? They will not suffer. Any lesson that is designed by the teacher can be expanded or abbreviated to meet individual needs. Incidently, a student who has a difficult time with one skill such as sequencing may not have difficulty with another such as vocabulary development. With traditional grouping, a teacher would provide the same remedial instruction for all students in that group. With a whole class format, a teacher can address the needs of students as they pertain to the lesson. In other words, using whole class instruction allows a teacher to better individualize, allows a teacher to focus more on students and less on time management.

One of the hidden benefits of a whole class instructional method, however, is noticed most by students. It is the great pleasure students get from all sharing a story together. No turtles group, no bluebirds group. The increase in self-esteem these students will feel because they are no longer in competition is amazing.

Reading Buddies

Reading buddies is a way of grouping students into simple pairs to read a book. Each pair of students can do the reading together, work cooperatively on all follow-up lessons as the teacher sees fit and share the work load on projects and presentations. With reading buddies each pair need not be reading a different book. The pairing is only for the purpose of providing some of the benefits listed below.

A reading buddy system provides flexibility. Teachers can decide to what extent the students will work together. If one pair of students comprehends best when they hear the story, then the teacher can allow them to read their chapters to one another. On the other hand, students who read best silently can be paired together for follow-up activities and projects only. Pairings can be made between students of similar ability so that they advance at the same pace, or students can be paired to complement each other. This method is flexible enough to allow the teacher to decide.

Another advantage is the amount of individual time the teacher can spend with each student or pair of students. With students working together, teachers are free to meet with each pair and check progress. Several times a week each buddy pair can meet with the teacher for *quality time* that allows the teacher to work on that pair's particular need.

Although teachers experience real advantages with this system, the students are the big winners. First of all reading buddies allow more student-to-student interaction. All too often we see students focusing only on the teacher in a classroom. In the student's mind it is the teacher who has all the right answers. Thus, when a class discussion develops, some students tune out the comments of their classmates. A system of reading buddies turns that behavior around. It forces students to work, discuss and even read with a student partner, and they learn to listen and work with that other student. Discussion skills improve because students are able to express themselves in a more risk-free setting.

Reading buddies also allow for more individual pacing. With students working in small pairs, the teacher is free to let students advance at their own pace. Students who normally have a difficult time with comprehension can be paired together in order to take the pressure off of them to keep up and reduce their frustration level.

Conversely, students who normally eat up every bit of reading can move along at their pace. These students will have more time to work on the extension of the lessons.

What I really like best about this system is the way it encourages students to become more responsible for their own education. Instead of being led through a book or story by the teacher, students can work cooperatively with each other as they are guided by their teacher. Students learn to budget their time and when they really get interested, they are free to forge ahead. Personally, I'd rather be chasing them through the reading experience instead of dragging them.

Some pitfalls do exist with this system. Classroom quiet is usually the first casualty. At any one moment several pairs of students may be reading aloud while another pair is discussing an activity, and still others are moving about the room as they do project work. It may not be quiet, but it should not be chaotic and disruptive. I have found that as students use this system, they learn to adjust their voices and noise level down while increasing their ability to keep their attention focused on the task. After the first few days of learning to adjust the volume, students get on track and stay on track longer.

Grouping Students

Although I would not advocate a strict grouping by ability as the only method of developing a reading format in a classroom, grouping by ability is desirable given the right circumstances. Those *right circumstances* depend on the students with whom you're working and most of all the literature you're using. Some stories are long or have an advanced vocabulary or are written in a style that makes it difficult to understand. This type of literature is demanding and requires a student who is more proficient in those reading skills. In those cases a teacher will want to put together a small reading group whose level of development best fits that literature.

It is equally important, though, to realize that it is possible to divide students into reading groups that are not based on ability, but on other factors. One of those other factors could be interest.

I have had classes (and so have you) in which I know that a certain book would interest certain children but not others. Under those circumstances, it is right to allow students to read those stories they would naturally find more interesting. Another way might be to present the books for the next unit to the students and allow them to express which books they think they would prefer. (This can be done privately in order to prevent students from just trying to hook up with their friends.) As the instructor you make the final grouping, but it would be done with their input which would provide additional motivation during the reading of the story.

Grouping by reading style is another option. Put all the auditory readers together and do more reading aloud. Get the visual readers in one group and give them time to read quietly. A group of tactile/kinesthetic readers would love to experience the literature by reading and doing, in some cases living the experience of the characters of the story.

Simply put, no one method of organizing students for reading is always best. As teachers, the last thing we need is to believe that there is one right way. What we all need are choices, and those choices will change from year to year just as the students in our classes change from year to year.

Reading Skills Developed in This Book

Comprehension

All the skills developed in this book ultimately lead to better comprehension at some level. The specific activities developed for "comprehension," however, target certain areas. They include recalling, verifying and evaluating.

Recalling	Requires students to remember key events that will assist them in understanding the story line. Students may be required to rely strictly on memory and then check their responses in the text of the story or may be asked to use the book in finding an answer. Strategies such as story maps, summarizing and webbing are used along with a question/answer format.
Verifying	Requires students to prove whether a statement about characters, the setting or the plot is true or not true based on the text. Students will need to locate and cite the proof they find.
Evaluating	Requires students to make judgements about the actions of the characters based on their own personal lives and support them with their own reasons.

Text Structure

Have you ever shuddered when asking students to locate a passage on a page because you know that in the end you'll have to show everyone where it is by pointing? Activities related to this section allow students to develop skills necessary to better move about the literature during discussion as well as better comprehend dialogue and narration.

Paragraph Identification	Activities may require students to locate an answer by identifying page and paragraph number.
Dialogue	Most literature includes narration as well as the dialogue of the characters. Activities are developed to get students to see the difference between these two. Other activities allow students to gain insight into the action of the story by noting the way characters speak through the *explanation words*. ("Get out of here," *he said in a low, threatening voice.*)

Vocabulary

This section of each lesson promotes the development of vocabulary in students. It will do so in a number of different ways. The traditional method of looking a word up in the dictionary is used on occasion but not extensively. It is impractical to expect students to sit down to pleasure read with a dictionary at their side. More often students do what we do when we come to an unfamiliar word in text, they read past it. If it is not crucial to the understanding of the story or episode, it is forgotten. If it is necessary, however, then they need strategies to help them decipher it. These strategies include the following:

Context Clues	Students are expected to figure out the meaning of the word based on meaning clues found within the sentence or paragraph. Students learn that they may have to read ahead or go back and reread a previous passage in order to find the clue to understanding a word.
Word Parts	Students are expected to decipher a word based on its recognizable parts. This may involve compound words or words with prefixes and suffixes. Students are also asked to identify the base word in order to better understand the meanings of words that appear in other forms.
Selecting a Most Appropriate Definition	Oftentimes we are confronted with words that have more than one definition. Some vocabulary activities will have students choose the definition that best fits the way the word is used in the story. Students will be required to go back to the text of the story to verify that definition. Homonyms are occasionally included.

Sequencing

This is the ability of the student to correctly arrange key events or episodes into their correct chronological order. Activities involving this skill will get students to identify clue words that help them correctly see the proper sequences as well as see the story as a whole.

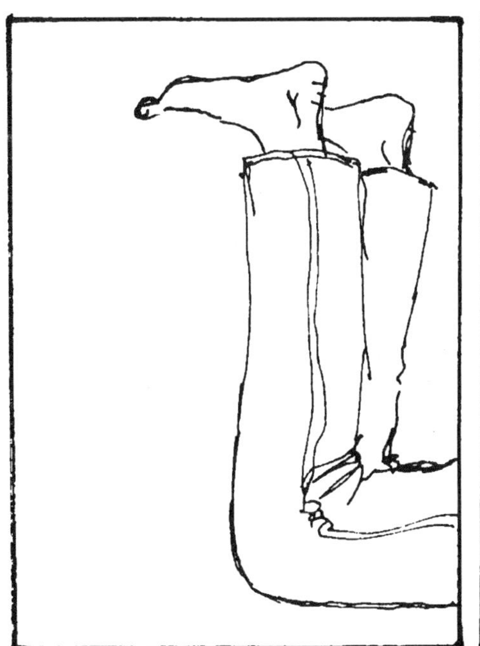

Higher Level Thinking Skills

Four specific areas are developed for each piece of literature. These activities may come at the end of the book or at the end of an episode.

Predicting	Requires students to forecast what may happen next in the story or what would have happened if a key event or element in the story were changed.
Planning	Requires the student to develop a sequential plan related to an episode in the story. An outline of duties in developing the plan is provided.
Decision Making	Requires the student to imagine he is a character in the story and support a decision the character made or develop and justify a different decision.
Productive Thinking	Requires students to think creatively and to develop many different and usual alternatives to a given situation in the story.

Identifying Story Elements

Every story has the same elements (setting, character, plot and theme). Students will not only be introduced to these elements but will see how the author develops each and weaves it into the story.

Setting	Students will identify both the time and place of the episodes and the story in general. They will trace setting changes and understand how the setting contributes to the plot of the story.
Character	Students will have the opportunity to trace main characters in the story from the time they are introduced through their development in the story. Activities will allow students to draw conclusions about the personalities of these characters and verify those conclusions based on the text of the story.
Plot	This refers to the action of the story. The plot of a story is often broken up into episodes. These episodes may encompass part of a chapter, a full chapter or several chapters. Students will be able to map the development of the plot through the different episodes.
Theme	When a specific theme or lesson is presented in a story, students are asked to identify it and find instances from the story that support that theme or lesson.

Cause and Effect

This is the ability of the student to see logical cause and effect relationships in the story. Activities involving this skill will get students to not only identify cause/effect and effect/cause relationships but will also get them to develop their own cause/effect relationships all within the context of the story.

Fact and Opinion

This is the ability of the student to distinguish between statements of fact and statements of opinion. Activities involving this skill will get students to make judgements as to whether the statement given by a character in the story is a reflection of fact or opinion.

Identifying Figures of Speech

In literature, where it can be found, students will have the chance to identify and then develop their own figures of speech such as similes or personification. A definition and example of each introduces the section.

Maps, Charts, Graphs and Diagrams

As extension exercises, students will have the chance to more clearly visualize the setting of each story by drawing or illustrating scenes or objects from an episode using maps and graphs.

Other extension activities may have students preparing a presentation to the class or reading group. Developing charts or graphs to assist in the presentation is explained.

How to Use This Book

This book has selected literature that students find exciting and interesting to read by authors they want to read over and over. The literature selected is written for students in the third through seventh grades.

It takes that literature and prepares lessons that will help you, the teacher, guide your students through the book while reinforcing good thinking and reading skills. You'll find vocabulary, comprehension, reading skills and enrichment lessons for episodes of the literature the students are reading. It is not a prescription. You will want to pick and choose what activities you want students to do according to their level of reading development.

The important thing is that you will have a choice. You'll have ready-made materials available if you want to work on simple recall with a certain chapter, or sequencing, or even higher level thinking skills. The lessons are all there. In fact a list of all the reading skills developed for the literature is included in this book.

In addition, if you feel you want to work on a skill not developed in the lesson sections of this book, you need only to model any of a number of formats in preparing the materials for your students.

The chapters for any one of the titles have been organized into reading units. Many units are one chapter in length. Some may be two chapters and a few are more than two. In combining chapters into one reading unit, I took into consideration the size of the reading assignment it would entail and how well those chapters formed one episode of the book.

The lessons for each reading unit follow a simple pattern. Most chapters have a Before You Read section which provides an activity that will prepare students for the reading. It may get them to reflect on what they have read already or help them relate what they are about to read to their own lives. Each chapter also has an As You Read section. This is a short paragraph that instructs students to focus their attention on certain aspects of the reading. The final section is After You Read. This section is filled with activities that allow students to exercise their reading skills in a way that specifically pertains to the chapters they've just read. Interspersed between chapters are higher level thinking skill activities as well as projects. All activities and projects have been placed where I thought they best fit the story. You may want to use them elsewhere.

The Extension Activities at the end of each title's lessons are explanations of other projects you may want to undertake. Be sure to look through Extension Activities from titles you are not using in order to get additional ideas.

When using a book in the classroom, no chapter should be "activitied" to death. In fact in my classes we frequently read a chapter together with no activity lesson accompanying it. Of primary importance is to get children reading and enjoying the literature. The lessons are there because they are going to help students become more effective readers, more relaxed readers and eventually more independent readers.

Howliday Inn

by James Howe

Harold and Chester live a safe and comfortable life with the Monroe family. All of that comes to an end when the Monroes take a week-long vacation and board the two animals at a kennel known as Chateau Bow-Wow. Upon arrival they find out that Dr. Greenbriar will be on vacation. In his stead two apprentices, Jill and Harrison, will be attending all the "guests" for the week. These guests include Max, an athletic dog; Louise, a jealous poodle; Georgette, a Southern belle of a poodle; Taxi, a mutt of doubtful mental capabilities; Lyle, a totally flipped out cat; Heather and Howard, two wire-haired dachshunds who mysteriously avoid others; and, of course, Chester and Harold. Although Harold doesn't seem to mind the idea of being boarded, Chester is his usual suspicious self. Even before arriving, he is convinced that no good will come of this experience.

The mystery begins almost immediately when the two are dropped off. Louise is in the process of throwing a fit because she is convinced Max was flirting with Georgette. The next day the argument continues but encompasses Lyle who had jumped on Louise mistaking her for a bombing target. In the following argument, Lyle seriously threatens Louise. All this tension comes to a head when Louise is found missing the next morning. Although Jill is convinced it is her fault for leaving the gate open during the previous night's storm, Chester begins an investigation because he believes that Louise did not just run away but was kidnapped. Chester's not-too-subtle detective work results in his announcement that he knows who the kidnapper is. Before he can reveal the identity, however, Chester turns up missing.

It is now left to Harold to solve the mystery. He first finds out that Chester was killed when Jill accidentally dropped some poison that was meant to be thrown out. He continues his investigation but comes up with more suspects than clues. First Max and Georgette disappear, then Heather and Howard. That night following a terrible nightmare, Harold is awakened by none other than Chester, who we learn had not been poisoned but kidnapped. The two of them along with Taxi and Lyle set out to save the real victims of the kidnapper, Heather and Howard. Heather, it turns out, is about to deliver a litter of pups and Harrison is out to get them . . . for profit. In the end the animals do stop Harrison in time for Dr. Greenbriar and Jill to apprehend him.

Note to the Teacher:
This is an excellent book to introduce the theme of mystery. The story line is easy to follow, clues are noticeable and the characters, although mostly animals, are well developed and very entertaining. Younger students may not understand some of the subtle humor in the dialogue but can still follow the plot. The vocabulary will present a problem in places, but the most difficult words and expressions will not stop students from understanding what is happening. The vocabulary activities included in this book plus your own expertise will offset any problem the vocabulary may impose.

Name________________________________ Date________________

Chapter 1: Howliday Inn

Before You Read

Vacation. Just the word brings a smile to almost anyone's face. A regular vacation away from school is nice, but a traveling vacation can be even better. Think of all the wonderful places to go, things to see and things to do.

Don't forget all the things that need to be done before you go on a trip. Going on a trip requires quite a bit of planning. You have to plan where you're going, what clothes to take, how you're going to get there and what to do about any extra responsibilities you have such as a paper route or pets. Then there is the garbage that has to be taken out, newspaper and mail need to be handled, and what about the lawn and garden?

Imagine you are going to go on a traveling vacation. Prepare for that trip by drawing a set of plans that will allow you to go.

Use the Planning Work Sheet in order to plan a one-week traveling vacation. Don't go anywhere too far. After all, you have only one week. You will need to consider three things:

1. Where you will be going and what you will need for the time that will be spent traveling in the car
2. What you will be packing for your stay
3. What you will have to do around the house to get ready for the time away

Name____________________ Date__________

Planning Work Sheet

Step One: The Destination

You have one week for your vacation. You will be traveling by car. Remember to allow for traveling time and choose a destination. You may want to use a map.

I plan on going to ______________________________.

We will be traveling in the car about ______________________________.

The things I will need in the car to pass the time will be:

______________ ______________ ______________

______________ ______________ ______________

______________ ______________ ______________

Step Two: Packing

The second step is deciding on what to pack. You will want to consider the weather, what kinds of things you will be doing when you get there and how many days you will be spending at this place. With all this in mind, list all the items you will pack and how many of each item you will need.

______________ ______________ ______________

______________ ______________ ______________

______________ ______________ ______________

______________ ______________ ______________

______________ ______________ ______________

______________ ______________ ______________

Step Three: Getting Things Ready Around the House

You cannot just pick up and walk out of the door when you go on vacation. You have to let certain people know you are leaving, cancel things for the week you are gone, take care of any responsibilities like pets or jobs. If you play on a team, you have to take care of that responsibility.

On your own paper, list all the extra responsibilities you have to take care of before you leave. After each one, explain how you are going to take care of that responsibility.

Name________________________________ Date________________

Chapter 1: Howliday Inn

As You Read

The first chapter of any book is very important. It is in the first chapter that we are introduced to the three important parts of any story–the setting, the characters and the plot. As you read Chapter 1 you will want to pay attention to all three. Each one is described below. Use the questions to help guide you through the reading in Chapter 1.

Setting

The setting of a story is when and where the story takes place. The setting may change from chapter to chapter and may even change within a chapter. It is important to pay close attention to any changes in the setting as you read.

In *Howliday Inn* the story begins in one place. We soon find out that the rest of the story will continue in another place. Read to find out when and where the story begins.

1. When does the story take place? Does this story take place in the distant past (many, many years ago), the present or the distant future (many, many years from now)?

   ____

2. Where does this story take place? Where are the characters of this story in Chapter 1?

   ____

3. Where are the characters of this story headed at the end of Chapter 1?

   ____

4. The dog and cat are going to be staying in one place for a week. Do you think this place is going to be good or bad for them?

   ____

   On the lines below tell why you think this way. Write in complete sentences.

   ____

   ____

   ____

   ____

Name____________________________ Date________________

Chapter 1: Howliday Inn

Characters

Did you ever wonder what a pet would say if he/she could talk? How would a fish describe what it sees on the other side of its fish tank? What opinions would a cat have about its family? What activities would a dog say it enjoys the most?

In this book most of the characters are animals. In many ways they act like humans. They talk to each other. Each one has its own personality. Each one has its own likes and dislikes. In Chapter 1 you will be introduced to two of these animal characters, a dog and a cat.

1. What is the dog's name?____________________________
2. What is the cat's name? ____________________________

3. List the names of the human characters introduced in Chapter 1.

____________________ ____________________

____________________ ____________________

Personalities

It is important to think of the characters of a story as real people. Real people have personalities. They can be talented, friendly, mean, cowardly, brave, noble, jealous, etc. The characters of a story are the same way. In this book the dog and the cat both have personalities.

Based on what you've read so far, what kind of personality would you give the dog and the cat? On the lines below list two to five personality traits for each one and be ready to explain why you wrote each one down.

The Dog:

_______________ _______________ _______________

_______________ _______________

The Cat:

_______________ _______________ _______________

_______________ _______________

You will be meeting many more animal characters as well as human characters in this book. For each one it is important to figure out what kind of personality he/she has.

Name________________________________ Date________________

Chapter 1: Howliday Inn

Plot

What happened?

The plot of the story is what happens in the story. It is not only the main events of the story but also all the details. As you read, it is most important to keep track of the main events of a story. Because this is a mystery story, you will also want to keep track of the details. It is in the details of the story that you will find clues to the mystery.

To make sure that you understood the main events of Chapter 1 as well as some of the details, answer these questions.

1. Why was Toby so upset at the beginning of the chapter? ____________________

   ____

2. When Harold first learns what is going to happen, what is his biggest worry?

   ____

3. What is Chester's opinion of being boarded? ____________________

4. What are three things about being boarded that Chester worries about?

   a. ____

   b. ____

   c. ____

5. How does Chester try to get out of being taken to the boarding place?

   ____

6. What is Chester's final warning to Harold as they are leaving?

   ____

Name________________________________ Date______________

Chapter 2: Howliday Inn

Before You Read

Chester really is upset about going to Chateau Bow-Wow. He's convinced that it will be a dreadful place with lots of very strange animals. Of course, Chester does seem to be the kind of cat that is very hard to please. In fact, you have to wonder if any kennel would be good enough for him.

See if you can imagine a kennel that even Chester would enjoy. On the lines below list five or six of the things that would be in this kennel that would please Chester.

______________________ ______________________

______________________ ______________________

______________________ ______________________

Now in the space below diagram what this "kitten palace" would look like. Be sure to label everything that you draw so that the reader of your diagram can tell what it is and where it is located.

As You Read

It's time to see if Chester's feelings about this place are true. Read to find out what kind of place the Chateau Bow-Wow is. In addition, you will be introduced to some new characters. Read to find out who these characters are and what their problems are.

Name________________________________ Date______________

Chapter 2: Howliday Inn

After You Read
Vocabulary

Base Words

A base word is a word to which a beginning (prefix) or an ending (suffix) has been added. Sometimes if you do not know the meaning of a word that has a suffix or prefix added to it, you can figure it out by first figuring out what the base word is.

Example: When Harold is upset in Chapter 1, he whimpered pitifully. You may not know what *pitifully* means, but knowing that the base word is *pity* will help you to figure out that *pitifully* means that Harold cried in a way that would make Mr. Monroe feel pity or sympathy for him.

With this in mind, write the base word for each of these words that can be found in Chapters 1 and 2.

Chapter 1

1. fitful ____________________
2. fateful____________________
3. contentedly ________________
4. sensibly __________________
5. uneasy ___________________
6. carrier ___________________
7. insensitive ________________

Chapter 2

8. reassuringly _______________
9. resounded_________________
10. fiendish __________________
11. unimpressed_______________
12. aback____________________
13. sullenly __________________
14. drily_____________________

Now comes the hard part. Using the base word, try to figure out which definition is the best by circling it. You will also have to go back to the chapter and find the word in order to see how it was used in the sentence.

1. fitful: restless and full of tension **or** full of good health
2. carrier: a box used to carry an animal **or** a small car
3. fiendish: in a very friendly way **or** in an evil sort of way
4. resounded: to clear your throat before speaking **or** to make a long, repeating sound
5. drily: sounding like a drill **or** to say something in a dry, sarcastic way

Name____ Date____________________

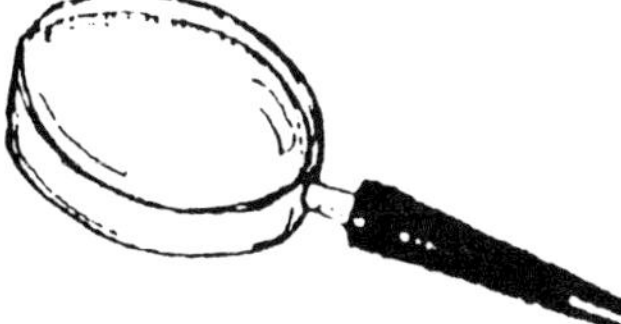

Chapter 2: Howliday Inn

The Detective's Handbook

Part One: Who's Who at Chateau Bow-Wow

In Chapter 2 you were introduced to a few more characters. Three of them were dogs and three of them were humans. Each of the three animals seemed to have his own personality, but they also shared a problem. It is too early in the story to begin looking for suspects, especially since no crime has been committed yet. It is not too early, however, to begin keeping a list of characters with a little bit of information about each one. A list like that may come in handy if something mysterious does happen.

For each of the characters introduced in Chapter 2, write down some information. You should include information that you know as well as opinions that you are forming about each one. Hang on to this list as you read the story. You can add to it as you learn more about each one.

Harold and Chester are done for you as examples.

Harold: A dog, no certain breed. He will be staying at Chateau Bow-Wow for about one week. Likes chocolate cupcakes, gets car sick, seems kindhearted and friendly, average intelligence.

Chester: A cat, no certain breed. He will also be staying at Chateau Bow-Wow for one week, but he's upset about being there. He thinks something bad will happen. He thinks he is quite smart. He reads. He does not seem very friendly, and he does not seem to trust anything new. Harold and Chester will be boarded next to each other.

	Name	**Information and Description**
1.	______________	______________________________
2.	______________	______________________________

Name________________________________ Date________________

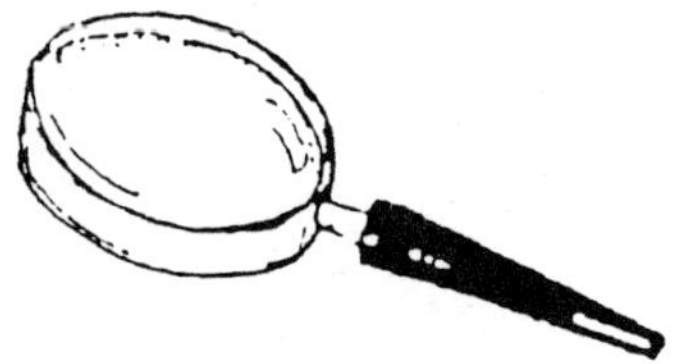

Howliday Inn

Who's Who at Chateau Bow-Wow

3. ______________ ____

____

____

____

____

4. ______________ ____

____

____

____

____

5. ______________ ____

____

____

____

____

6. ______________ ____

____

____

____

____

Name______________________________ Date__________________

Chapter 3: Howliday Inn

As You Read

A good plot involves conflict. Conflict is when there is a problem between two or more characters. In Chapter 2 you saw conflict among Louise, Max and Georgette. As you read Chapter 3, notice how that conflict gets even bigger. Also notice that a new conflict begins. Read to learn between what two characters this new conflict is and what the new problem is.

After You Read

Detective Handbook

In this chapter you were introduced to two more characters, Taxi and Lyle. In addition to that, you get more information about Max, Louise and Georgette. Take the time to add to your list of Who's Who at Chateau Bow-Wow.

Description Words

In telling this story, Harold uses a lot of words to describe how people talk. For example, in Chapter 2 Pete said good-bye to Harold *sarcastically,* and Louise argued *relentlessly.*

Notice that both these words end in *-ly*. Use your ability to skim the pages to find out how the different characters spoke and acted. Match Column A to Column B by placing the correct letter in the space.

Column A

A. cooly

B. absently

C. thoughtfully

D. blankly then quizzically

E. politely

F. gruffly

G. sadly

Column B

1. ______ How Jill looked around when Harrison asked her if she'd forgotten anything
2. ______ How Harold introduced himself to Max
3. ______ How Max spoke when he found out Harold didn't jog
4. ______ How Max talked to Taxi when he asked how Taxi was doing
5. ______ How Taxi nodded at Harold when he was introduced to him
6. ______ How Max spoke when he talked about poison, drowning and stabbing
7. ______ How Lyle stared at Louise when he told her he didn't like being crossed

Name____ Date____________________

Chapter 3: Howliday Inn

After You Read

Memory Buster

With your book closed, try to answer these questions. When you are done, open your book, check your answers by filling in any missing ones and putting the page number where the answer was found in the space next to the question.

1. What was happening when Harold awoke the first time? p. _____

____

2. Jill said Harrison blew hot and cold. What does that mean? p. _____

____

3. Why were Jill and Harrison letting the animals out of their bungalows? p. _____

____

4. What was it that Max wants Harold to do that Harold can't do very well? p. _____

____

5. What did Taxi see on a television show that seemed to interest Max? p. _____

____

____

6. Why does Louise get mad at Max again? p. _____

____

____

7. What does Louise say to Lyle that causes him to threaten her? p. _____

____

____

Super Trivia Question

How does one get into the storage shed?

____

Name____ Date____________________

Chapter 4: Howliday Inn

Before You Read

There seems to be quite a bit of tension in this special boarding house for dogs and cats. Louise is jealous of Georgette and therefore mad at Max. Max is fed up with Louise. Louise is fed up with the way Lyle acts, and Lyle is threatening Louise. It sounds confusing, but it could also be dangerous for someone if this tension is allowed to erupt.

Being upset with people is normal in our lives. We get mad at others when they don't act the way we think they should or don't do the things we want them to do. In Chapter 3 we saw how some of the characters handled their tension. They argued with each other, yelled at each other and even threatened each other.

How do you handle tension? Do you argue and yell? Do you keep quiet and just let the tension build up? Do you fight? Do you get mad and walk away in a huff? Maybe you go upstairs and punch your pillow. There are many ways of handling tension and anger, and chances are you do different things depending on the situation.

Try to recall a time when you got mad at someone. It would be a time when you felt really tense. On the lines below describe what happened in a few sentences.

____

____

____

Now explain what you did to handle your tension or anger.

____

____

Looking back on it, do you think that was the best way to handle your anger? On the lines below explain another way you could have handled your anger. See if you can think of a way to handle anger that will not hurt anyone but still allow you to feel better. Be ready to discuss this in class.

____

____

As You Read

In this chapter we will witness some more conflict, only this time it is between two humans. Read to find out what problem Harrison and Jill have and notice how Harrison acts and how Jill acts.

Name______________________________ Date________________

Chapter 4: Howliday Inn

After You Read

Detective Handbook

In this chapter you were introduced to Heather and Howard. Add them to your Who's Who at Chateau Bow-Wow list. Also in this chapter you got a better look at Harrison and Jill. It's time to add them to your list, too. Pay particular attention to the way Harrison and Jill treat each other and the animals. That could be important.

Cause and Effect

An interesting game is stacking dominoes. If you set them up just right, they will all fall down when you knock over one. Cause and effect thinking is just like that. One event occurs and it causes another to occur which in turn causes another and so on. Read the beginning of each sentence below. Finish it by writing what should come after the word *because*. You may have to look back through all the chapters you've read to find some of the answers.

Example: Harold and Chester had to stay at a pet boarding house *because*

the Monroe family was going on a long vacation.

1. Jill and Harrison have been left in charge of Chateau Bow-Wow *because*

____

2. Louise is mad at Max and Georgette *because*

____

3. Lyle threatens Louise *because*

____

4. Chester thinks Heather and Howard are werewolves *because*

____

5. Harrison often criticizes Jill *because* he says she is

____

Name______________________________ Date________________

Howliday Inn

The Detective's Handbook

Part Two: The Compound

In Chapter 2 Harold and Chester were taken to the boarding house. In that chapter the area where the pets are kept is described. That area is called the compound. Then in Chapters 3 and 4, more of the compound is described when the animals are out talking with each other and when Jill and Harrison are working. A good thing for a detective to do is to map out the area so that when a crime is committed he or she can better visualize what happened. With a partner find those episodes in Chapters 2, 3 and 4 where you are told what the compound looks like.

When you are done with that, use those episodes to create a diagram of the compound with your partner. Your diagram should have a title; it should have all the bungalows drawn and labeled; the gate and office should be included and labeled as well as the shed and anything else you read about.

Use the space below to sketch your first draft. Then on a piece of clean paper prepare your final sketch complete with color, title and labels.

Name____ Date____________________

Chapter 5: Howliday Inn

Before You Read

So far in this mystery you have had the chance to hear the thoughts of only a few of the characters. Harold is telling the story so, of course, we know what he has been thinking. Chester, Harold's friend, has told him everything he is thinking; so we know Chester's thoughts too. Louise is very upset and a very outspoken poodle. She's been so mad that she has told everyone her thoughts . . . quite loudly. The characters you haven't really heard from yet are Max, Taxi and Georgette.

All that you know about these characters is the little bit of talk they have had with each other. You have to wonder what they are really thinking.

Choose one of these animal characters and try to imagine what he or she is really thinking. Imagine what he or she thinks of Harold and Chester; what he or she thinks of Harrison and Jill; what he or she thinks of Louise, her temper and her jealousy; what he or she thinks of the entire Chateau Bow-Wow.

On the lines below write what you imagine are the thoughts of the character you chose. Write these thoughts as if that character were actually thinking them. Be ready to share your writing in class.

____

____

____

____

____

____

____

____

____

____

As You Read

Chester feels that the growing tension between the animals and people at Chateau Bow-Wow is going to explode. In this chapter we find out he is right! Read to find out what terrible crime has been committed.

Name____________________ Date____________

Chapter 5: Howliday Inn

The Detective's Handbook

Part Three: Making a Chart of the Suspects

When he thinks a crime has been committed, a good detective makes a chart of all the suspects. Below is the outline of that chart. It is really simple. It lists all the possible suspects in one column. After each one it leaves blocks to write in information about his motive and any important evidence or information. You are to fill in the chart as completely as you can. The more you are able to write about each suspect, the better able you will be to figure out the crime.

Use the definitions below to help you understand what goes in each block. You will certainly want to reread parts of Chapters 2, 3, 4 and 5 in order to get as much information as you can. You will also want to reread most of Chester's conversation with Harold. It is Chester, after all, who thinks everyone is a suspect.

Save a little space to add more information later when you read other chapters.

Suspect: anyone who you think may have committed the crime

Motive: the reason why someone would want to commit the crime. In real life, a person cannot be found guilty of a crime unless there is a reason why that person would want to do it. No motive = not guilty of a crime.

Evidence/Information: anything that helps you figure out who committed the crime. For example, the unlocked gate is a piece of evidence and Lyle's threat is a piece of information.

Suspect	Motive	Evidence/Information
1. Max		
2. Taxi		
3. Georgette		

The Detective's Handbook

Suspect	Motive	Evidence/Information
4. Heather and Howard		
5. Lyle		
6. Jill		
7. Harrison		

On the lines below, write a short paragraph in which you explain what you think happened. Was it murder? Was it kidnapping? Is Louise just a runaway? Make a decision and write your reasons. Be ready to share them in class.

____

____

____

____

____

____

____

____

____

____

____

Name________________________________ Date________________

Chapter 6: Howliday Inn

As You Read

Chester really seems hot on the trail of a criminal . . . if a crime has been committed, of course. In this chapter you will get more evidence and information that will help you to figure things out. Read to find out what Chester discovers as he snoops around.

After You Read

Detective's Handbook

You got a little more information in this chapter about some of the suspects. Add that information and evidence to your chart. Does it change what you thought after Chapter 5? Be ready to discuss what you think happened to Louise after considering this new information.

Context Clues

Some words have more than one possible definition. When you're reading and come across one of these words, you may not know which definition is meant. In order to figure it out, you may need to pay attention to how the word is used in the sentence or paragraph.

Below are nine words with two possible definitions after each one. Find each word and read carefully the way it was used in the sentence or paragraph. Circle the definition that best fits the way it was used.

Chapter 5

1. distress: in need of assistance **or** feeling worried or tense
2. countered: to answer back **or** to count money on a table
3. forlorn: a pitiful look **or** deserted or abandoned
4. pensive: filled with ink **or** in deep thought
5. cahoots: a loud howling **or** working together with someone
6. abated: to take away an amount of money **or** not as strong

Chapter 6

7. eavesdrop: to listen secretly to others **or** part of a roof
8. glowered: to stare at someone angrily **or** a bright smile
9. faze: a stage of development **or** to bother or disturb

Name______________________________ Date________________

Chapter 7: Howliday Inn

Productive Thinking

Before You Read

Ever since you were old enough to remember, you have been getting warnings. Don't touch this; don't touch that. Stay away from over there. Never talk to strangers. Watch your step; look where you're going. The list is probably endless.

Take a moment to remember all of the warnings and advice that you've gotten in your life from the time you were a young child.

On your own paper list many common and unusual warnings and bits of advice that you have received. Be ready to share some of these in class.

At the end of Chapter 6 Chester gave Harold a most unusual warning. Harold was told to stay awake and not to go to sleep. It is not likely that you ever got that kind of advice!

Chester must have had a reason for recommending such a strange thing. What do you think he was thinking?

On your own paper list many different and unusual reasons why Harold should stay awake all night. Think about what he might see if he does stay awake. Think about what he might miss if he falls asleep.

When you are done, get with a buddy and compare your ideas.

1. Put a check by the ones that are alike.
2. Put a star by the ones you think might really happen.

Name______________________________________ Date____________________

Chapter 7: Howliday Inn

As You Read

In Chapter 6 Chester really stuck his neck out by telling everyone that he knew the truth about what happened to Louise. Someone could be out to get Chester now! Of course maybe Chester really does have an overactive imagination as Max said. Maybe Louise really did just walk out to get back at Max.

Read Chapter 7 to find out what Chester knows or to find out what happens to Chester.

After You Read

Sequencing

Below are ten sentences from the story you are reading. Put them in the order in which they happened by writing a 1 in front of the sentence that tells what happened first, a 2 in front of the sentence that tells what happened second and so on. Do this with the book closed, and put your answers in the first set of spaces. Then check your answers and make any changes in the order in the second set of spaces.

_____ _____ Louise is found missing in the morning.

_____ _____ Louise and Max get into another argument that ends with Lyle threatening Louise.

_____ _____ In the morning Harold finds that Chester is missing from his bungalow by listening to Jill and Harrison's conversation and learns that Chester was poisoned.

_____ _____ Harold and Chester witness the first argument between Max and Louise.

_____ _____ Chester talks to Harold about all the possible ways and reasons that Louise is missing. Taxi hears them accuse him.

_____ _____ Chester and Harold are taken to Chateau Bow-Wow to stay while the Monroe family is on vacation.

_____ _____ Chester and Harold eavesdrop on Georgette and Max but are discovered when Chester falls onto their doorstep.

_____ _____ Harold meets Howard and Heather, the wire-haired dachshunds, and Chester says he suspects that they are really werewolves.

_____ _____ Chester announces to everyone that he knows what has happened to Louise.

_____ _____ On a stormy night Jill and Harrison forget to feed the animals and in the confusion Jill forgets to close the gate.

Learning About Suspense

One of the elements of a mystery is suspense. Any "who done it" ought to be suspenseful just because the reader wants to solve the mystery. Really great mystery writing, however, is suspenseful for two more reasons. First, it is suspenseful because of the way the writer makes the plot twist and turn. The second way it can be made suspenseful is by the way the author is able to use language to create images in the reader's mind. As part of a discussion you will want to introduce this element of suspense and take a look at the way James Howe has helped to build it.

An easy definition for *suspense* is "a feeling the reader gets when he or she does not know what is going to happen next in a story."

Suspense in the Plot

In discussion you can have the students identify the suspenseful moments in each chapter. This can be done as a whole group or in pairs. It can be done as each chapter is read or at this halfway part in the story. Regardless of the format, have them focus on things that happen that lead us to believe that something will go wrong even though we don't know what it is. Below are some chapter-by-chapter events that helped build suspense.

Suspenseful Moments

In Chapter 1 we get Chester's warning that there is trouble ahead. That begins the suspense.

In Chapter 2 we learn that Dr. Greenbriar will not be tending the animals as expected, and instead two helpers of suspicious ability will be in charge. We are also introduced to the main conflict, Louise and Max. In both cases we are led to feel that something is going wrong, but we don't know what will happen.

In Chapters 3 and 4 the tension with Louise escalates and a new conflict (with Lyle) is introduced. His warning at the end of Chapter 3 really helps turn up the suspense, and the uncertainty over Howard and Heather's howling adds to it too.

Chapter 5 has Louise missing for no easily explained reason.

Chester's nosing around in Chapter 6 only leads to more conflict that almost bursts wide open when everyone descends on Harold's bungalow. At one point in this chapter we don't know whether everyone has come to "get" Chester for his snooping around or not.

The real coup de grace of suspense, however, is when Chester comes up missing (presumed dead) right after he warned Harold that big trouble was coming. At this point we don't know "who done it."

Suspenseful Activities

To help students understand this suspense even more, you can have them chart it out chapter by chapter on a large wall chart or overhead transparency. Entitle the chart "Suspenseful Moments," and as a group or in pairs have students identify some of these key events. This activity is best done cooperatively in a small group or pairs format. Discussion is facilitated this way allowing students to build on each other's ideas. I do not recommend just making this an individual "seatwork" assignment.

Younger readers who cannot relate to the idea of suspense can still learn to identify these events. Instead of calling it "Suspense," entitle the chart "Mysterious Clues," and tell students to find clues in each chapter that lead them to believe that something mysterious is going to happen.

By doing this activity intermittently, you can have students predict what will happen next. Their predictions can be kept on another chart and added to their detective handbooks. As a math extension you could also graph their predictions by keeping count of how many students make the same predictions and turning those numbers into a bar graph.

Suspenseful Writing

First Sentences

The other way James Howe helps build suspense is through the imagery he creates with words. This can be easily brought out by having students read the first line of each chapter from one through seven. In each case we are catapulted into the suspense of the chapter in just one or two sentences.

As an activity, you can begin by having students read and discuss why each of these opening sentences creates such a strong image in our minds. Then have them illustrate some of the images that that one sentence conjurs up.

Another extension activity along these lines is to have each student write his/her own powerful first sentence. In class students can read their sentences and discuss how each one might be turned into a story line. This discussion can be done in small groups or in pairs. Eventually some of these ideas can be turned into a complete story with students pairing up to coauthor the story.

A variation is to have the teacher create several "first sentences" which students must extend into a story or an opening to a story. Students select the first sentence they want by bidding on it. What do they use for bidding? How about the number of sentences they will write in developing the sentence into a story or opening? The more a student wants a certain opening sentence, the more he/she will be willing to write (or bid) in order to get it. You can set the minimum bid. You can also have them work in pairs.

Illustrations are a natural for this lesson. A lesson on captions would precede any drawing students would do. You or the students can bring in newspaper or news magazine pictures complete with captions that help to describe the pictures.

The next step is to have students look at illustrations in *Howliday Inn* or any other book they've read and have them add captions to those illustrations.

Finally, they reverse this idea by providing the illustration for the "powerful first sentence" that they created. Magazine cutouts can be added to help make their illustrations more vivid.

Suspenseful Settings

The setting is another strong image that is developed in *Howliday Inn*. The "dark and stormy night" idea really comes through in this story. In discussion have students focus on why a storm at night is such an effective mystery setting. You may want to also point out that the storm isn't just a nighttime thing. It continues throughout the story.

The dark and stormy night is not the only mysterious setting. Have students brainstorm for other spooky or mysterious settings. You can even integrate this with social studies by having students select mysterious settings in history (for example, a dark and deserted cathedral during the Middle Ages, nighttime outside the newly built pyramid around 1500 B.C.). Another angle is to have them list scary and mysterious settings in their neighborhood. (For example, the vacant lot at the end of the street, the deserted apartment house two blocks away, their school late at night.)

Begin by having them focus on a time and place. Don't worry about having them describe the place in writing right away. That comes next.

Through discussion, each of their settings can be expanded. Examine how James Howe builds his rainy setting with words like *pelted* to describe the rain or *streaked* to describe the lightning. Students can keep a log of especially effective words.

Eventually, students can begin to integrate some of this language into their own writing. Using the settings they imagined, allow them to write paragraphs that describe those settings.

You can even make a game out of it by having students underline creative, descriptive words they used in their paragraphs. Point totals are then awarded based on how well the settings are developed. Individuals or writing teams with the highest point totals win.

Book covers of their settings can be designed, colored and displayed complete with titles of the imaginary books. Each book cover can be done by a different student or pair of students who will base the drawing on the descriptive writing.

If artistic ability is a problem, magazine cutouts can replace some of the drawings with the students adding their own accents around the pasted on magazine pictures. (For example, the spooky cathedral scene described above could be made by cutting out a picture or photocopy of a cathedral and pasting it onto the paper. Dark clouds or a full moon could then be easily drawn by the student around the cutout.)

Name________________________________ Date________________

 Chapter 8: Howliday Inn 

As You Read

Poor Harold! Poor Chester! This vacation is not going very well. Rotten weather can make it hard to enjoy a vacation, but poisoning will ruin it every time.

In this next chapter Harold gets over his grief long enough to take on some detective work of his own. Read to find out what Harold learns during his own investigation. Also, when you are done reading, decide whether you think Harold is as good a detective as Chester.

After You Read

Vocabulary

What Do They Mean?

Our language is full of phrases that don't really mean what they say. For example, if you ask for someone's help and they say, "No, I'm all tied up right now," they don't mean they have rope around them but that they are too busy to help. These special expressions have a name. They are called idioms.

Harold likes to use idioms when he talks. In Chapter 8 he used quite a few. See if you can figure out what these expressions mean by finding them in Chapter 8 and explaining what they mean by rewriting the sentences you find them in.

For example, if the idiom was "in hot water," you would have to look through the chapter until you found the sentence with that expression in it. Now imagine you found the sentence and it read, "I'm really in hot water now," said Harold. You would rewrite the sentence so that the idiom was replaced with its meaning. You would write, "I'm really in trouble now," said Harold. The idioms have been listed in the order they are found in the chapter.

1. off the track____

____

2. a slippery devil ____

____

3. on the ropes ____

____

4. chewing the fat____

____

5. get off your chest ____

____

Name______________________________ Date________________

Chapter 8: Howliday Inn

After You Read

Prove It

A good detective doesn't draw a conclusion without some proof. That is what Harold tries to get in Chapter 8. Unfortunately, he gets very little proof when he goes out to investigate. Let's help him out. Below are sentences about some of the suspects in this missing person crime wave. See if you can find some proof. Write the page number where you found it. The more proofs you find, the better.

1. Prove Max and Georgette like each other.

____

____

____

____

____

2. Harold calls Lyle an oddball. Prove that Lyle is an oddball.

____

____

____

____

____

3. Prove Heather and Howard are acting suspiciously.

____

____

____

____

____

Name____________________________________ Date____________________

Chapter 9: Howliday Inn

Before You Read

Secret Messages

Harold has a secret message he has to figure out. It could solve the mystery! Making up secret messages can be a lot of fun. All it takes is a little bit of imagination to come up with a secret code.

One way of making a secret code is to make every letter of the alphabet stand for another letter. See how Harold's secret message looks using the code below.

YAXD YWLXM WVE GWL

A	B	C	D	E	F	G	H	I	J	K	L	M	N	O	P	Q	R	S	T	U	V	W	X	Y	Z
Q	I	Z	U	A	P	B	Y	O	H	N	X	C	G	W	D	F	K	M	E	V	R	L	S	J	T

Another way of making a code is to write everything backwards. Harold's secret message would look like this if that code were used:

WON TUO SLWOH PLEH

If you want to make that code a little tougher, separate all words into groups of two letters. Harold's secret message would then look like this:

WO NT UO SL WO HP LE H

Still another way to make a code is to write it without any vowels. Harold's message looks like this with that code:

HLP HWLS T NW

Using one of these codes, write a secret message in which you tell who you think is doing these terrible things and why. Share it with a reading buddy.

____

____

Just for fun, come up with your own secret code. Write the same message you wrote above with that code and be ready to share it in class.

As You Read

In this chapter Harold works at solving the mystery of the message but discovers an even bigger mystery while doing so. Read to find out what has happened in Chateau Bow-Wow that has Harold and Taxi very confused.

Name______________________________ Date______________

Chapter 9: Howliday Inn

After You Read

Memory Buster

After you've read this chapter and feel you understand it, close the book and see what you can recall about it from memory. Don't look in the book until you have answered as many questions as possible. When you are done, open your book and check the answers you've written. Put the page number where you find that answer in the space after the question. Fill in any missing answers.

1. In Harold's message, who does he think "howls" is? p. _____

 ____

2. Who does Harold see running through the compound during the storm? p. _____

 ____

3. Who else has Taxi seen running around that night? p. _____

 ____

4. Who has been left in the compound? p. _____

 ____

5. In his dream what did Harold constantly hear? p. _____

 ____

6. Who appeared in Harold's dream? p. _____

 ____

7. Who appeared in Harold's bungalow after Harold's dream? p. _____

 ____

Name____ Date____________________

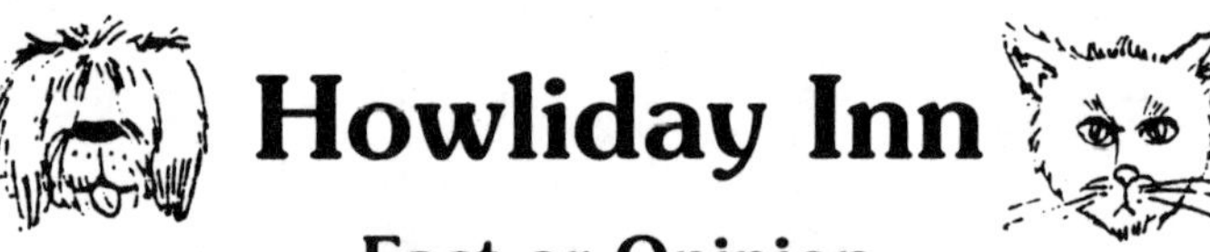

Fact or Opinion

Was Chester dead? Is Louise really gone? Are Max and Georgette guilty? How about Heather and Howard? Things really have gotten confusing. Everyone has an opinion about what has happened.

An opinion is an idea a person believes but can't prove is true. An opinion might also be someone's feelings about something or his judgement. For example, if a person thinks blue is the prettiest color, that is his opinion. In the story Chester thought Chateau Bow-Wow was a disgusting place to be boarded. That was his opinion because not everyone thought it was so bad. Harold thought Chateau Bow-Wow was pretty nice . . . to begin with. Opinions usually have judgement words like *good* or *bad*.

A fact is an idea that is true or can be proven true. For example, if you say you are wearing shoes and you can look down and see them on your feet, then it is a fact that you are wearing shoes. In the story it is a fact that Louise is missing. We know it is a fact because she is no longer in her cage; no one has seen her, and both Jill and Harrison have admitted she is missing. To say that she ran away, however, is an opinion because we just don't know what happened to her. We only know she is missing.

A reader of mysteries is always looking for the facts. By getting the facts he or she can usually piece together a solution to the mystery. Below are ten statements. You must decide which ones are facts and which ones are opinions. Put the letter *F* in the spaces before the ones that are facts and the letter *O* in the spaces before the ones that are opinions.

1. _____ Louise was kidnapped.
2. _____ The gate was open the morning Louise was found missing.
3. _____ Max and Georgette want to get Louise and Chester out of the way.
4. _____ Lyle hates Harold and Chester.
5. _____ Lyle threatened Louise.
6. _____ Jill and Harrison have been left in charge while Dr. Greenbriar is on vacation.
7. _____ Taxi is jealous of anyone that Max pays attention to.
8. _____ Heather and Howard are werewolves.
9. _____ Chester was poisoned because he knew too much.
10. _____ Georgette spends time with Max.

Name____ Date____________________

Chapter 10: Howliday Inn

As You Read

Chester's alive? Harrison said he was poisoned. This really is turning into a mystery. We can't even trust the characters who are supposed to be dead to stay dead. In Chapter 10 a lot of the mystery begins to unfold.

As you read, pay attention to what is happening to Heather and Howard. They are an important part of the mystery. Then read to find out why Chester has returned and to find out how the rescue attempt works out.

After You Read

Vocabulary

Base Words

Each word below is taken from Chapter 10. In the space after each word write its base word if it has one. You may need to look up some of the words in the dictionary to get the correct spellings of the base words.

Following each word are two definitions. Find the word in the chapter and then circle the definition that fits the way the word was used in the story. The words are listed in the order in which they appear in the story.

1. eerily: Does this word mean in a frightening way **or** echoing in a person's ears?
2. befuddlement: Does this word mean a confused look **or** a look of horror?
3. stealthily: Does this word mean to move toward something you want to steal **or** to move quietly?
4. queried: Does this word mean to act in a strange way **or** to question?
5. discarded: Does this word mean something made of cardboard **or** something thrown away?
6. amplified: Does this word mean to make bigger or louder **or** to make smaller or softer?
7. vehemently: Does this word mean with lots of expression; forceful **or** with care and understanding?

Name______________________________ Date________________

Chapter 10: Howliday Inn

After You Read

Cause and Effect

With cause and effect order, one event causes another to occur. Read the beginning of each sentence below. Finish it by writing what should come after the word *because*.

Example: Harold went back to his bungalow and fell asleep *because*

there was no one left in the compound to question.

1. Chester got Lyle and Taxi out of their bungalows *because*

____

2. Chester, Harold, Lyle and Taxi had to listen carefully *because*

____

3. Howard and Heather had gone to the discarded drainpipe *because*

____

4. Chester had everyone jump Harrison *because*

____

5. Harold began barking *because*

____

6. Dr. Greenbriar and Jill came to the boarding house *because*

____

7. Harrison had committed the kidnapping *because*

____

Name_______________________________________ Date____________________

Chapter 11: Howliday Inn

Before You Read

We now know the answer to the question "Who done it?" It is Harrison. That's fine but there are a lot of questions left unanswered–questions about Max and Georgette, Louise, Chester and even Harrison.

Below are some of those questions. Before you read Chapter 11, see if you can figure out some of the answers and put your thoughts on the lines.

1. Why did Harrison want to take Louise?

____

____

2. Where was Chester the whole time everyone thought he had been poisoned?

____

____

3. How do you explain Max and Georgette's disappearance that night?

____

____

4. Why did Heather and Howard always act so strange, almost unfriendly?

____

____

5. Was anyone else involved in the kidnapping? If yes, who? Why?

____

____

As You Read

In Chapter 11, all these questions and more are answered. Read to find out the full explanation.

Name________________________________ Date________________

Chapter 11: Howliday Inn

After You Read

Hopefully you now understand the whole mystery. Just to make sure, answer these questions in full sentences. Then compare these answers to the ones you wrote before you read the chapter to see how accurate you were the first time.

1. Why was Harrison kidnapping the animals?

   ____

2. How was Harrison able to kidnap Louise and Chester without Jill finding out? (two answers)

   ____

   ____

3. How did Chester learn about Harrison's plan?

   ____

4. How did Chester learn that Heather and Howard were the valuable ones?

   ____

5. What were Max and Georgette doing out? Who knew that all along?

   ____

6. Were Lyle and Taxi involved in the kidnappings in any way?

   ____

7. Why were Heather and Howard always acting so strangely?

   ____

Name________________________________ Date________________

Chapter 12 and Epilogue: Howliday Inn

As You Read

All stories have to come to a full ending. Although the mystery is over, Harold and Chester are not home yet. A good author always puts an unusual twist into the ending just for fun. Read to find out the unusual twist James Howe adds to the ending.

After You Read

One of the most important things to notice about this story is the way all the animal characters acted a lot like humans. Even when they did dog-type things, they had names for them which made them sound normal. For example, in Chapter 12 Max, Georgette and Louise leave to go play. Of course they don't play tag or baseball like humans would. They play dog games with names that make them sound realistic. On the lines below name the two dog games that they play.

______________________________ ______________________________

Now think about any other pet you've ever had or seen (bird, hamster, cat, fish). If they could talk what would they call their games? On the lines below write the type of animal and the name it would give one of its games. You should fill in at least two.

Animal	Name of Its Game
______________________________	______________________________
______________________________	______________________________
______________________________	______________________________
______________________________	______________________________
______________________________	______________________________
______________________________	______________________________

Supplemental Vocabulary

Not all the lessons contain vocabulary work. Nonetheless, you may want to supplement your teaching with additional vocabulary work from time to time. Below are additional lists of words by chapters. No more than seven words per chapter are included.

Chapter 1

1. befall
2. blissful
3. relieved
4. hysteria
5. subsided
6. dire
7. intrigued

Chapter 2

1. desolation
2. chap
3. endearing
4. veterinarian
5. bungalows
6. ranted
7. fare

Chapter 3

1. incessant
2. futile
3. coaxed
4. anemic
5. nuisance
6. overwrought
7. console

Chapter 4

1. retorted
2. identical
3. encased
4. scurried
5. exasperated

Chapter 5

1. bewilderment
2. flirting
3. detection
4. deliberation
5. investigation
6. deductions
7. accomplice

Chapter 6

1. incriminating
2. nameless
3. overstimulated
4. chortle

Chapter 7

1. vigil
2. dabbing
3. smock
4. recollection

Chapter 8

1. frolicker
2. culprit
3. vowed
4. bludgeoned
5. hunches
6. falter
7. respite

Chapter 9

1. caterwauling
2. scurrying
3. reverberated

Chapter 10

1. bade
2. dwell
3. intrusion
4. riveted
5. lunged
6. unruly

Chapter 11

1. nauseated
2. pored
3. dolt
4. heating duct
5. sleuth
6. purebred
7. dispose

Chapter 12

1. captive
2. tribute
3. abdominal
4. deprivation
5. berserk

Extension Activities

Reader's Theater

One of the strengths of this book is the development of the animal characters. Each character has a distinct personality and in some cases a distinct way of talking. In addition, the action of the story often focuses on a conversation between the characters. These two elements, strong characterization and well-developed dialogue, are excellent components for a reader's theater activity.

What Is It?

Reader's theater is nothing more than a method of presenting the action and dialogue of a story without all the movement and need for props and costumes that a play requires. In it students each take a part to play. Narrator can be one of these parts. After practicing, students perform an episode or scene from the book by reading it aloud to the audience. They do not have to memorize any lines. They hold their books the entire time. The performance comes in the development of the characters through the use of vocal inflection and facial expression.

How Is It Done?

The "actors" or readers face the audience during the entire performance. They never look at each other. All facial expressions and reactions to what the other characters are saying are directed at the audience. The audience then gets a front view of each character at all times. Students can make slight hand gestures if they wish, but it isn't necessary. Students do not have to wear costumes but can suggest a character with some small item (for example, a bow in the hair for Georgette).

How Do Students Prepare?

Stage One: Select the material. Students need to select a scene that relies less on action and more on dialogue. Good examples might be in Chapters 2 and 3 when Louise is arguing with Max and others or in Chapter 6 when Chester announces to everyone that he knows who the culprit is.

Stage Two: Choose characters and edit the script. How you choose who will play whom is up to you. You can have tryouts, lottery, volunteers, whatever works best. Editing the script involves getting everyone to eliminate unnecessary wording from the text such as all explanation words (for example, "...queried Harold" or "Max asked..."). Since the book is narrated by Harold, the part of narrator is just another character.

Stage Three: Rehearse the voices. Have students practice developing the distinct voice that will be that character (Louise with her French accent, Max with perhaps a tough-guy voice). Encourage creativity. Then have them rehearse reading the lines to each other at a table or in a circle. Get each voice to react to what is being said to him.

Stage Four: Rehearse for facial expressions. In this last stage students will sit or stand in a row and practice adding facial expressions as they read their lines. Remember to have the readers who aren't reading show a reaction to the lines of another character.

Language Development

1. Acrostic Poems

Have students create acrostic poems for each of the characters in the story. In this type of poem the first letter of a character's name is the first letter of a word or phrase that relates to that character.

For example:

Just clumsy
Inclined to cry
Lively and
Lovely

} Jill

2. A Book of Idioms

Once students come to better understand idioms, they can create their own books of idioms, individually or as a joint venture. To do this, students need only think of an idiom and then illustrate it. Of course, their illustration will be the literal definition of the idiom. For example, one idiom is "He's in hot water." The line could be a caption for a picture of a person waste deep in a kettle of hot water. The books by Ed Gwynn (*The King Who Rained*, *There's a Frog in My Throat*) are an excellent kickoff to this activity. A little string and a hole punch can turn these into humorous and entertaining books.

Creative Writing

1. Point of View

The entire story is told from Harold's point of view. Wouldn't it be interesting to hear from another one of the characters? Working individually or in teams, students can rewrite an episode of the story from Max's or Taxi's or anyone's point of view.

This assignment can include instruction on writing dialogue and the subsequent punctuation that goes with it. It also allows students to fabricate story parts creatively while relying on an already-developed script. I have found that students especially like sticking to the characterization of a particular character. Taxi remains a bit daft; Georgette retains her flirtatious ways but gets to explain her "intentions" in a way we never get from Harold.

2. In this story we get a chance to see what pets think of things they are subjected to by their masters. Students can extend on that idea by preparing a paper on how another pet sees his/her life. Any pet would do (fish, hamsters, lizards, hermit crabs, mice, birds, etc.). Begin by brainstorming for subtopics such as playtime, favorite foods, daily routine and things humans do that drive me crazy. The composition can include one or more of these topics. The paper is then prepared as if the pet were actually doing the writing so that we can read what he is actually thinking.

Variation

Have students prepare an interview with this pet. All questions and answers are written out and rehearsed in advance. The entire production can be designed like a talk show with one talk-show host and several animals all responding to the questions. Videotape the production and send it home for the night with each participant when you've finished.

3. **Who's Howie?**

In the last chapter we are briefly introduced to a new character, Howie. This is the dachshund that the Monroe's adopt. This is a character with no developed personality. Students, working in teams or individually, can work to create a personality for Howie. Have them develop an episode involving this young dog's doings once the Monroe's get home.

Students will need to decide on a personality for the dog (enthusiastic and energetic or quiet and shy, special speech patterns, etc.), a situation or problem for the episode, involvement for the other animals, even a solution to the problem. Setting will also need to be developed. This activity gives students an opportunity to practice what they have learned in reading.

Reports

If you're interested in some reports for your students, here are some possible topics.

1. **Pet Care**

Students prepare reports on the care of particular pets. Brainstorm for subtopics such as feeding, living quarters, costs, breeds, etc. Set the parameters of the reports to suit the grade and developmental level of the students. When possible, have a culminating activity in which the students bring in their pets as part of oral reports to the class.

2. **Careers**

What does a veterinarian do? How about someone who runs a kennel? Dog groomers? Detectives? Students will need to contact someone firsthand with this topic. Subtopics include schooling needed, skills required, cost to establish a business, equipment that is needed and, of course, duties of that career.

3. **Dog and Cat Breeds**

We are never really told what breeds some of these characters are. Chester could be a Persian cat or a Minx. Different breeds could be assigned or selected. Subtopics could include history of the breed, physical traits, training, caring and grooming, etc.

Variation

On the creative side, students could prepare interviews or reports in which the animal breed speaks and acts as the students would expect that breed to act. For example, a German Shepherd with a German accent whose business is as a guard dog or police dog, a very stiff and proper English Setter, a slow-moving bloodhound. If students are not ready to work at this level, a class discussion on that topic would suffice.

The Egypt Game

by
Zilpha Keatley Snyder

One summer, eleven-year-old April Hall comes to live with her grandmother in an apartment house while her mother pursues a career as a movie star. Resentful and angry, April develops an unfriendly and bitter attitude that makes her a difficult person to get to know. Despite these oddities, she befriends Melanie Ross and learns that they have something wonderful in common, huge imaginations. Together with Melanie's tag-a-long brother, Marshall, they discover a deserted storage yard behind a neighborhood store and begin to remodel it into the ancient land of Egypt where they can carry out extravagant, made-up ceremonies.

Just after school begins they meet another new boarder in the apartment house, Elizabeth Chung. Although two years younger than both girls, Elizabeth proves she too has an imagination worthy of the Egypt game and soon becomes a part of the troupe.

The girls and Marshall spend almost all their free time designing a temple, statues, ceremonies and even beginning a hieroglyphic alphabet before tragedy strikes. Another girl in the neighborhood is killed by an unknown assailant. Even though their parents still know nothing of the Egypt game, the children are forbidden to play outside. One of the chief suspects in the killing is the professor who owns the store and storage yard in which the Egypt game takes place. The professor is a very private and rather unfriendly man so everyone suspects him. Eventually, things cool off, and just before Halloween the girls make plans to return to "Egypt" on Halloween night. They do so and are followed by two boys, Toby Avillar and Ken Kamata. Upon discovering the girls' game, the boys agree not to tell anyone if they too can play.

Now the six Egyptians continue to develop the Egypt game complete with an oracle ceremony designed to answer questions about the future. Astoundingly, the oracle works and now the Egyptians begin to think that perhaps they have created their own sort of monster. Even though Toby admits to having tampered with some of the questions, there are still unexplained events which have them all guessing.

One night when April is baby-sitting Marshall, she returns to the storage yard land of Egypt to retrieve a book. While exiting, she is attacked by the assailant and would have met with an untimely end had the professor not been watching and begun yelling for help. The assailant is caught. At the police station and later at the apartment house, the Egypt gang learn that the professor was watching their game all along, acting as a secret guardian. The experience brings April and her grandmother closer together, destroys all suspicion surrounding the professor and leads to a more permanent friendship among the Egypt gang.

Note to the Teacher:

This book provides all the elements of a mystery in a not-too-scary plot. Excellent for fourth and fifth graders, this book will have the students guessing "who done it." Although the vocabulary level is rated as sixth grade, I have not found it to be too difficult for nine and ten-year-olds.

Name______________________________ Date________________

The Egypt Game

The Discovery of Egypt

Before You Read

Your neighborhood. You probably don't give it much thought. It's where you live. Everything is familiar–the people, the places, houses, apartments, schools and parks. Maybe because it is so familiar, you really don't notice how much there is to it.

Before beginning the book, *The Egypt Game*, take a little bit of time to think about your own neighborhood. Complete each section of questions below. Be ready to share your ideas in class.

Places

What is your street address?

____

What is the best "get away" place in the neighborhood for you?

____

Where's the best place in the neighborhood for a game with lots of your friends?

____

Do you have a place in your neighborhood to buy things? What is its name?

____

People

List one to three of your friends that live in your neighborhood.

__________ __________ __________

Name an adult in your neighborhood that is friendly with everyone, even the kids.

____

How does this person show friendliness?

____

Is there anyone in your neighborhood whom you consider to be mysterious or someone you try to avoid? Explain who and why.

____

____

Name______________________ Date______________

The Egypt Game

The Discovery of Egypt

As You Read

Every story has three things in common: a setting, characters and a plot. The setting is when and where the story takes place; the characters are the people in the story; the plot is what happens in the story. So where does the mystery come in? Not all stories have mystery but *The Egypt Game* does.
The story begins in a neighborhood. But this neighborhood has a place that is a little strange, a little curious. This neighborhood has a person that is also a little strange. Read to find out who and what is mysterious in the neighborhood of *The Egypt Game*.

After You Read

Setting

The setting of the story is when and where the story takes place. The setting may change from chapter to chapter and may even change within a chapter. It is important to pay close attention to any changes in the setting as you read.

In *The Egypt Game* the entire story focuses on one neighborhood. The setting changes are the different places within the neighborhood. In order to better understand the settting of this story, answer the questions below.

1. When does the story take place? Does this story take place in the distant past (many, many years ago), the present or the distant future (many, many years from now)?

   ____

2. In what month does the story begin?______________________

3. Where does the story take place? Does the story take place in a city (apartment houses and stores), the country, (farms and open land) or the suburbs (rows of houses with an occasional school and park)?

   ____

4. What place in the neighborhood is particularly mysterious?

   ____

5. Why is this place so mysterious?

   ____

   ____

Name____ Date____________________

The Egypt Game

The Discovery of Egypt

Characters

The characters are the people of the story. Not all the characters have to be people. In fact you may have read some stories where animals or ghosts were the characters. So far in this story, however, the characters are people.

On the lines below list the names of the characters who have been introduced.

____________________________________ ____________________________________

____________________________________ ____________________________________

Put a star by the character who is most mysterious.

Plot

The plot is what happens in the story. It is not only the main events of every chapter but also the details. As you read, it is most important to keep track of the main events of a story. Because this is a mystery story, you will also want to learn to pay attention to the details. It is in the details of the story that you will find clues to the mystery.

To make sure that you understand the main events of this chapter as well as some of the details, answer the questions below.

1. Where was the professor when he witnessed the beginning of the Egypt game and what was he doing? ____________________________________

   ____

2. How did the two girls and boy manage to get into the professor's backyard?

   ____

3. What was in the backyard that inspired the girls' imaginations?

   ____

4. Why could the children not see the professor, but he could see them?

   ____

   ____

Name______________________________________ Date________________

The Egypt Game

Enter April/Enter Melanie and Marshall

Before You Read

Think for a moment about a friend of yours. Picture that person in your mind. This person could be someone around your age or someone much older than you. Write his/her name below.

____

A Fun Time

Now think of something fun you did with that person. It could have been a shopping trip, going to a movie, a game you played, etc. On your own paper tell about that fun time. When you are done, label this brief story #1.

When the Two of You Met

Can you remember how you met this friend of yours? Was it in school? Was it in the neighborhood? Maybe you were on the same team or maybe he/she moved into your neighborhood. On that same sheet of paper that you wrote story #1, skip three lines and tell about the time you met your friend. Explain how you met and your first impression. Describe your friend. When you are done, label this brief story #2.

Read Your Stories

Now you will need to get together with someone and read your two stories to each other. Have one person read both stories before the other person reads both stories. Be sure to read them in the order that you wrote them (#1 and then #2).

Think

Was the order that you read the stories the most logical way? ____________________

What other order could you have read the stories, and why would it have been logical to read them that way?

____

____

____

Name_______________________________________ Date____________________

The Egypt Game

Enter April/Enter Melanie and Marshall

Flashback

It may have seemed a bit unusual to read your stories in that order, first telling what you did with your friend and then telling how the two of you met. It would be more logical to first tell how you met your friend and describe the person and then tell about a fun time you had recently. In fact if you were going to combine the two paragraphs into one story, you may have wanted to do just that.

By reversing the order, you created a *flashback*. A flashback is when an author begins a story or episode and then suddenly goes back and tells about something that happened before the episode. In other words he "flashes back" to a time before the episode.

The two chapters you are about to read are flashbacks. They tell about events that occurred before Chapter 1.

As You Read

As you read these two chapters keep in mind that they are flashbacks and read to find out what kind of information we get in these two chapters. Ask yourself, "What have I learned in these two chapters that helped me understand the story better?"

After You Read

Like most flashbacks, the flashbacks in these two chapters give us important background information. We learn about April, Melanie, Marshall and a whole group of people. On your own paper, fill out the information about each character as it is asked.

April

1. Why has April come to live with Caroline?
2. How long might April be staying with Caroline?
3. Describe April's appearance.
4. Prove April is not happy to be living with Caroline.
5. Prove that April does not seem to like or trust grown-ups.
6. What special interest does April have?
7. What has Melanie heard about April before meeting her?

Caroline

1. How is Caroline related to April?
2. Why do you think Caroline does not take an interest in April's hairdo or other things?
3. What sacrifice has Caroline already made for April?

The Professor

1. What kind of objects does the professor have in his shop?
2. Prove that the professor is not very sociable.
3. What talent does the professor have that April admires?

Dorothea

1. What is Dorothea's relation to April?
2. What is Dorothea's relation to Caroline?
3. What is Dorothea's profession?
4. What happened to her husband, April's father?
5. Why did Dorothea have April move in with Caroline?

Melanie

1. How old is Melanie?
2. What unofficial job does Melanie have in the apartment house?
3. Prove that Melanie has patience with April.
4. What is Melanie's favorite type of game?

Marshall

1. How old do you think Marshall is?
2. What does Marshall carry around and why?

Character Traits

Describing a person involves more than telling what the person looks like. It also involves telling what his/her personality is like. A person's personality is made up of character traits like friendliness, stubbornness, quick temperedness, sense of humor, etc. On the lines below list some more character traits that you see in people you know.

_______________ _______________ _______________

_______________ _______________ _______________

List some character traits for April or Melanie.

_______________ _______________ _______________

_______________ _______________ _______________

Now Write

On your own paper write a description of the person you chose. Include a description of what he/she looks like and a description of his/her personality. Be ready to read it in class and most of all explain why you decided on those character traits.

Name________________________________ Date________________

The Egypt Game

The Egypt Girls/The Evil God and the Secret Spy

As You Read

In these two chapters the flashback catches up with the rest of the story. The girls find "Egypt." As you read these chapters, notice how much imagination the girls have. Read to find out how the girls mix their own imagination with what they've learned about ancient Egypt to create their own world. Also find out what special problem Melanie decides she has to solve before school begins.

After You Read

Vocabulary

Base Words

A base word is a word to which a beginning (prefix) or an ending (suffix) has been added. Sometimes if you do not know the meaning of a word that has a suffix or prefix added to it, you can figure it out by first figuring out what the base word is.

Example: In reading about Casa Rosada, we found out that Caroline's apartment *fronted* the avenue. You may not know what the word *fronted* means, but if you knew that the base word was *front,* you could probably figure out that Caroline's apartment faced the avenue.

With this in mind, write the base word for each of the words listed below that are in these two chapters. Remember that the spelling of the base word may change when a prefix or suffix is added. Use a dictionary to check your work.

1. sympathetic ____________________
2. accumulated ____________________
3. impressions ____________________
4. trimming ____________________
5. casualness ____________________
6. uncomfortable ____________________
7. donation ____________________
8. warily ____________________
9. defiantly ____________________
10. soberly ____________________

Your Turn

Now see if you can find your own. Look through any of the chapters you've read and find five more words that have prefixes or suffixes added to them. On your own paper list them. After each one, write its base word and the page number on which you found it. Be ready to share these in class.

Name________________________________ Date________________

The Egypt Game

The Egypt Girls/The Evil God and the Secret Spy

After You Read

Drawing Conclusions About Characters

So far in the story you've had the chance to meet many different characters but none seems so complicated as April. She dresses differently, she acts differently and she's got Melanie worried. Why is she like this?

Below are some of the things April says and does in these two chapters. Read them over.

1. April is having nightmares about school.
2. She puts on a Hollywood act around other children.
3. She narrows her eyes around grown-ups and talks sarcastically.
4. April wears eyelashes all the time and gets angry if asked about them.
5. She feels that Caroline doesn't believe Dorothea is going to come and get her even though Caroline has never said so.
6. She has a tremendous imagination.

How do you explain these things? What is causing April to act so nice sometimes and so nasty other times? On the lines below write a paragraph that explains April's behavior, nightmares and great imagination.

____

____

____

____

____

____

____

____

____

____

____

____

____

____

Name________________________________ Date________________

The Egypt Game

Eyelashes and Ceremony/Neferbeth

Before You Read

Beginning a new school year is exciting all by itself. Beginning a new school year at a new school can be exciting and scary too. On the lines below, list all the things about starting a new school year at a new school that would worry you.

________________________ ________________________

________________________ ________________________

________________________ ________________________

If you were in Melanie's place and wanted to help a new kid get through those first few days, what would you do? On the lines below list some things you could do to help a new kid get used to a new school.

________________________ ________________________

________________________ ________________________

________________________ ________________________

Knowing April the way you do, predict three problems that you think she will have as a new kid in school. Below each one predict how you think Melanie will try to help her through that problem.

1. ____

1. ____

2. ____

2. ____

3. ____

3. ____

As You Read

In these two chapters April tries to fit in as the new kid in school. Read to find out how it turns out. April isn't the only one who has to get used to a new school, though. Read to find out what other new character must get used to a new school and if she is allowed into the Egypt game.

GA1388

Name______________________________ Date________________

The Egypt Game

Eyelashes and Ceremony/Neferbeth

After You Read

Finding Details

A detail is a small piece of information in a story. Sometimes several details can be put together to help explain a general idea. For example, to say that the A-Z store was filled with unusual things could be backed up with the following details:

1. It had old-fashioned telephones, sewing machines and other appliances.
2. It had ancient statues from faraway places.
3. It had exotic objects like vases and knives with carved handles.

Each detail helps to explain the general idea that the A-Z was filled with unusual things.

Try to find two or three details for each general sentence below. Write them in the spaces.

A. April made it hard on herself to fit in at school.

1. ______________________________
2. ______________________________
3. ______________________________

B. After a while, April did things that helped her to fit in.

1. ______________________________
2. ______________________________
3. ______________________________

C. April and Melanie used many "found" objects to decorate Egypt.

1. ______________________________
2. ______________________________
3. ______________________________

D. Elizabeth's appearance and behavior made her easy to like.

1. ______________________________
2. ______________________________
3. ______________________________

Name________________________________ Date________________

The Egypt Game

Prisoners of Fear

As You Read

There comes a time in every mystery when something happens that is not explainable. That happens in this chapter. Read "Prisoners of Fear" in order to find out what terrible thing happens in the girls' neighborhood. Also find out who is suspected and why.

After You Read

Memory Buster

After you've read this chapter once, close your book and see what you can recall about it from memory. Don't look in the book until you have answered as many questions as possible. When you are done open the book and check all the answers you've written and try to find the answers you've missed. Put the page number where you found the correct answer on the space next to the question.

1. Why did Elizabeth fit into the Egypt game so well at first? p. _____

   ____

2. What caused the children to stop playing their game so suddenly one day? p. _____

   ____

3. What terrible thing had happened in the neighborhood? p. _____

   ____

4. Who did many people in the neighborhood suspect? p. _____

   ____

5. What happened to this person's store? p. _____

   ____

6. How did the children occupy their time since they could no longer play outside? p. _____

   ____

7. What has happened to Dorothea during this time? p. _____

   ____

Name______________________________ Date________________

The Egypt Game

Prisoners of Fear

After You Read

A Detective's Notebook

A good mystery is built on good, logical thinking and clues. In this chapter we've gotten a little of both. Use your own ability to think logically and identify clues to answer the questions below as you now begin to try to solve the mystery of the murder.

1. List everything you know about the crime that was committed.

_______________ _______________

_______________ _______________

_______________ _______________

_______________ _______________

2. List any suspects to the crime.

_______________ _______________

_______________ _______________

_______________ _______________

3. The professor immediately became one of the chief suspects (at least to the people around the neighborhood). List any clues or reasons as to why you think he could have done it.

____

____

____

4. List any clues or reasons why the professor may not have done it.

____

_______________ _______________

____

Name__________________________________ Date__________________

The Egypt Game

Summoned by the Mighty Ones/Return to Egypt

Productive Thinking

Before You Read

In creating their Egyptian costumes, the girls were pretty creative. They relied on objects that they found to make crowns, tunics and decorations.

A plastic bowling ball pin together with a cutout bleach bottle became a crown. Pillowcases and old sheer drapery became tunics. Cardboard and construction paper along with donated jewelry became decorations. Although these costumes would be used for the Egypt game, they would also make the perfect Halloween costumes.

It can often be hard to come up with a costume on Halloween. Sometimes it's easier to just go to the store and buy a costume, but the best costumes are homemade.

All of the Egypt costumes were made from found objects. It was just a matter of "seeing" something different in everyday, ordinary objects. Your classroom and school are full of everyday ordinary objects that could be made into costumes. Just think about some of the supplies you use in your class as well as playground equipment, etc. It just requires some imagination and being able to "see" something different in the ordinary.

Using the Productive Thinking Planning Sheet, list many different and unusual costume items you could make using ordinary objects you find in the classroom and school building.

Name____ Date____________________

The Egypt Game

Productive Thinking Planning Sheet

Step One: List the Objects

On the lines below list five ordinary objects found in your classroom and school building. Since you will be imagining how to use these objects, you are free to list any object you want.

______________________ ______________________ ______________________

______________________ ______________________

Step Two: Think Productively

Now comes the fun part. Each of these objects could be turned into something else. You are free to imagine that you can cut them, color them, and do anything you want to change them into things that could be a part of a costume. Remember, you do not have to change one item into a complete costume. You only have to imagine many different and unusual ways to change that item into something that could be part of a costume. The real trick is to come up with more than one idea for each item.

On your own paper, write the name of each item and after it list as many creative costume ideas as you can for that item.

Step Three: Visualize

Now that you are done thinking productively, look over your list of ideas. Some of them seem better than others. Put a star by the three best.

Using those three ideas, draw a picture of the costume idea to show others. Make it into a diagram with the items labeled. If you would have to cut or change the item at all, show how that would be done. Be ready to share these in class.

As You Read

It has been a while since April, Melanie, Elizabeth and Marshall have made it back to Egypt. April isn't the type to just wait patiently. She's not afraid to bend the rules a little in order to get what she wants. In these two chapters she does just that.

Read to find out how the "Egyptians" use Halloween to figure out a way to return to Egypt. Notice whose idea it is, who wants to back out and who doesn't find out until the last minute.

Name______________________________ Date________________

The Egypt Game

After You Read

Cause and Effect

"One thing always seems to lead to another." You may have heard someone say that at one time or maybe you've said it yourself. It is a really true statement. One thing usually does lead to another. In fact one thing often causes another thing to happen. That's the way it has been in this story so far.

April came to live in the Casa Rosada *because* her grandmother moved in order to give them more living space. Imagine how the story would be different if her grandmother had never made that decision.

Below are several cause and effect sentences as they relate to the story so far. Read the beginning of each sentence and finish it by writing what should come after the word *because*.

Example: April came to live in the Casa Rosada *because*

her grandmother wanted to make sure they had enough living space.

1. Melanie met April *because*

   ____

2. The Egypt game got started *because*

   ____

3. The girls were able to get into the back of the professor's yard *because*

   ____

4. The Egypt game had to stop *because*

   ____

5. The "Egyptians" were able to return to Egypt *because*

   ____

Name______________________________ Date________________

The Egypt Game

Egypt Invaded/Elizabethan Diplomacy

Before You Read

Egg crates and birdbaths are just a few of the objects the Egyptians have gathered to make the temple they call Egypt. It was very realistic in the daytime, but in the night it was just about enchanting. Can you remember all the other things they used to create this temple?

On the lines below list all the objects that the Egyptians made to create the temple. You may have to use the book to sort out a complete list.

________________________ ________________________

________________________ ________________________

________________________ ________________________

________________________ ________________________

________________________ ________________________

In the space below draw a diagram of what you imagine the temple to look like. You don't have to accurately draw each object. You can use shapes to represent different objects. Be sure to label each one.

As You Read

Every daring act has its risks. In these two chapters the worst nightmare of the Egyptians comes true. Read to find out who discovers the Egyptian game and what the Egyptians do to try to keep it a secret.

Name______________________________ Date________________

The Egypt Game

Egypt Invaded/Elizabethan Diplomacy

Vocabulary

Context Clues

Sometime words have different definitions and when you go to look them up in the dictionary you don't know which one to use. In order to select the right definition, you only need to look at the way the word was used in the sentence and match the most likely definition with the way it was used.

The words below are all in the two chapters you just read. After each one are two likely definitions for the word. Only one is the definition that fits the story. Use your book to locate the word, see how it is used in the sentence and select the correct definition. Circle the letter of the correct definition. Next to the definition that you circled, write the page number where you found the word used. The words are listed in the order you would find them in the chapters.

Egypt Invaded

absently: A. not present; not there
B. without thinking

parroted: A. to repeat exactly
B. to walk like a parrot

stalked: A. to walk in a stiff unnatural way
B. to move in a mean and threatening way

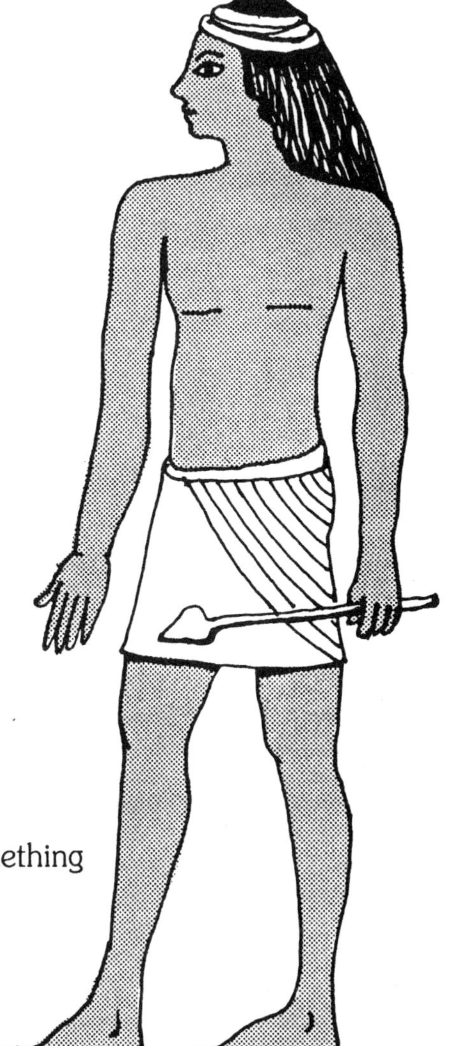

Elizabethan Diplomacy

angular: A. like an angel
B. full of sharp angles

fiendish laughter: A. laughter that is friendly
B. laughter that is evil or threatening

warily: A. in a suspicious way
B. to look at what a person has on

range: A. an area of open land for livestock
B. an area within which a person could be hit by something

console: A. to make one feel better; to cheer up
B. the cabinet of a radio or stereo

Name______________________________ Date________________

The Egypt Game

Egypt Invaded/Elizabethan Diplomacy

The story is just about halfway over, and it has begun to get a bit complicated. So before you get into the second half of the book, review everything that has happened so far.

Sequencing

Below are ten sentences from the story. Put them in the order in which they happened by writing a 1 in front of the sentence that tells what happened first, a 2 in front of the sentence that happened second and so on. Do this with the book closed and put your answers in the first set of spaces. Then check your answers and make any sequence changes in the second set of spaces. Be careful not to let the flashback confuse you.

_____ _____ Ken and Toby spy on the Egyptians during one of the secret ceremonies.

_____ _____ Melanie and April begin to read all about ancient Egypt.

_____ _____ April moves into the Casa Rosada.

_____ _____ Elizabeth is invited into the Egypt game.

_____ _____ April, Elizabeth and Melanie begin making Egyptian costumes.

_____ _____ A little girl is killed in the neighborhood and none of the children are allowed out to play.

_____ _____ The girls strike a deal with the boys. The boys will be allowed to play the Egypt game if they keep the whole thing a secret.

_____ _____ April hatches a plan to get back to Egypt on Halloween night when the chaperones aren't looking.

_____ _____ April explores the neighborhood and visits the professor's shop.

_____ _____ Melanie, April and Marshall discover the deserted storage yard that they turn into Egypt.

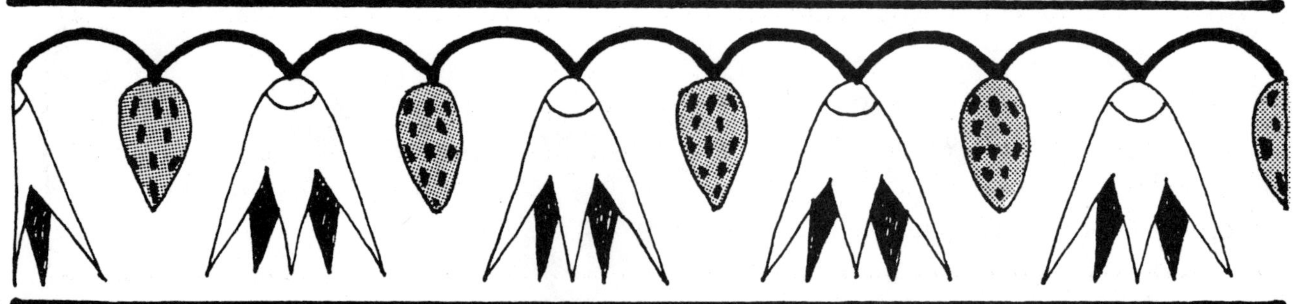

Name_______________________________________ Date___________________

The Egypt Game

Moods and Maybes/Hieroglyphics

Before You Read

Parents sure can be frustrating from time to time. Have you ever gone ahead and done something like a small job without being told because you thought it was the right thing to do only to find out that this time it wasn't? Have you ever asked for advice only to get a lecture? Have you ever asked if you could buy some clothes only to have one of your parents come along and buy the clothing you'd never want to wear? Sometimes parents are unpredictable.

Everyone has had an experience like that. It can lead to big arguments or just little ones, but it almost always is frustrating. Try to remember a misunderstanding you've had with your parents within the past year. On the lines below tell about it.

____

____

____

____

____

____

____

____

Now meet with someone in class and read your stories to each other. Listen to the other person's story carefully and when you're both done, see if you can imagine how each other's parents felt about that misunderstanding. Discuss how they would tell the same story.

As You Read

In the next two chapters Toby and Ken get more involved in the Egypt game. This does not happen, however, without problems. Read to find out what trouble Toby got into the night they discovered Egypt. Then find out how Toby and Ken add to the game and the argument that develops over hieroglyphics.

Name________________________________ Date______________

The Egypt Game

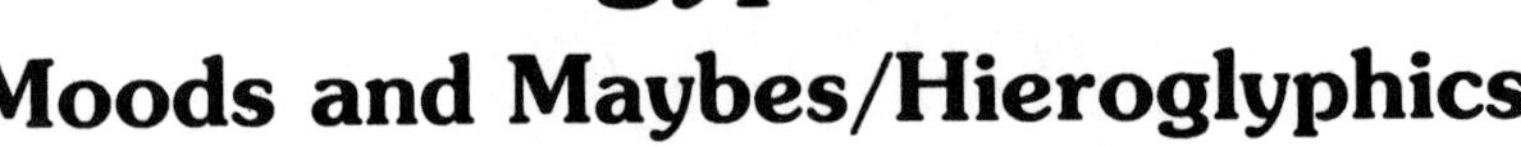

Moods and Maybes/Hieroglyphics

After You Read

Memory Buster

After you've read the chapter and feel you understand it, close your book and see what you can recall about it from memory. Answer each question below with the book closed. When you are done, check your answers. Do this by opening the book and finding the correct answer and putting the page number where you found the answer in the space next to the question. If you left any blanks, fill them in at this time in a different color pen or pencil.

Moods and Maybes

1. Why was Toby restricted until Friday? p. _____

   ____

2. Which parent was the first to get the idea to let the children out? p. _____

   ____

3. Who did Dorothea marry, and why can't April move in with her? p. _____

   ____

4. Which boy seems more genuinely interested in the Egypt game? p. _____

   ____

Super Trivia Question

Where are the secret scrolls hidden?

____

5. Which altar did the boys want to improve? p. _____

____

6. List three things they brought to improve that altar? p. _____

____

7. What was the first thing Toby thought they should do after the altar was fixed up? p. _____

____

8. Match the Egyptian name to the real person's name. p. _____

Elizabeth	Horemheb
Marshall	Aida
April	Marshamosis
Ken	Nefertiti
Melanie	Bastet
Toby	Ramose

9. Who works for Mr. Schmitt? p. _____

____

10. What was April and Toby's argument over? p. _____

____

11. What excuse did Toby use when other boys wanted to know where he had been going after school instead of playing basketball? p. _____

____

Super Trivia Question

Besides watching an anthill or the others play with hieroglyphics, what else did Marshall watch?

____

Name______________________________________ Date____________________

The Egypt Game

Ceremony for the Dead

Planning

Before You Read

Have you ever had a pet that died? It can be pretty upsetting. That's how Elizabeth feels right now. Her pet parakeet has died, and although it was only a bird, it was hers.

People have many different ways of taking care of dead pets–some have them buried, some take them to veterinarians who take care of them. Sometimes a family will even have a little ceremony in honor of the pet.

Ceremonies for the dead are common all over the world. Ceremonies for dead pets are not. Think what a ceremony for a dead pet should involve.

Begin planning a ceremony for a dead pet. Begin using the form below and continue on the next page. You will need to decide on the type of pet you are creating your ceremony for. Try to stick to a common pet like a cat, dog or bird, unless you have a different pet in mind that you once had.

Planning Guide Sheet

What type of pet will this ceremony be for? ______________________________

A ceremony for a dead pet could involve three steps. The first step would be a preparation step. The second step would be an honor ceremony. The third step would be the actual burial. (There are other methods besides burial, and you may want to plan for those instead.) Not all three steps need to be done. You will want to decide which steps to include in your ceremony. Read each of them over and decide which ones you want to include. Then design each one.

Name______________________________ Date________________

Plan the First Step

The first step is a preparation step. The animal and burial site have to be prepared. In addition, all materials have to be gathered. On your own paper outline your preparations.

1. Where will your pet be buried?
2. How will the burial site be prepared? List the materials and steps.
3. Will the pet need to be prepared? List the materials and steps.

Plan the Second Step

The second step is to plan an honor ceremony. An honor ceremony is a small gathering of people who pay their last respects to the pet. Use the steps below to help you plan the ceremony. Do this on your own paper.

1. Make a list of who should be present at the ceremony.
2. Decide where the ceremony should be held.
3. Decide how the ceremony area will be decorated and what materials will be needed.
4. Develop a short memorial service for the pet. Include who would speak at the service and what he/she would say. (You may want to prepare an actual script that they read or just prepare what topics each person should speak on.) Finally, if any prayers are to be said, they would also need to be decided.

Plan the Third Step

The last step is to plan the actual burial. Use the questions below to guide your planning. Continue working on your own paper.

1. Who will carry the pet to the burial site?
2. Will there be any decorations at the site? If so, list what they will be.
3. Will any special words be spoken just before the burial? If so, write what will need to be said. Also consider who will say these words and how they will know them.
4. Decide who will actually do the burying.

Name____ Date____________________

The Egypt Game

Ceremony for the Dead

As You Read

The Egypt game has really caught on with the boys, at least with Toby. It keeps getting more and more involved. Read this chapter to find out what kind of Egyptian ceremony they dream up for Elizabeth's pet bird. Focus your attention on all the different steps and procedures.

After You Read

Special Vocabulary

Below are some words associated with the ceremony for Prince Pete-ho-tep. Use your book to find each word and write the page number where the word was found. Then write a definition for each one in your own words and tell how it relates to the story. You may need a dictionary to help you out, but you have to put the definition in your own words.

Example: procession–p. ____– A procession is a group of people moving together in a straight line. The children formed a procession in taking Pete-ho-tep to the temple.

1. incense p. _____ – ____
____
2. bier p. _____ – ____
____
3. rites p. _____ – ____
____
4. mourn p. _____ – ____
____
5. wail p. _____ – ____
____
6. mummification p. _____ – ____
____

Name________________________________ Date________________

The Egypt Game

Ceremony for the Dead

After You Read

Step-by-Step

Making a pet parakeet into a mummified parakeet was a lot more involved than you probably imagined. Actually, Toby's research was pretty accurate. In some cases it did take over a month for the entire mummification process to be completed. So the week that it took the Egyptians of the Egypt game was really not that much.

The process of mummification was a step-by-step method preserving a body after death. The richer the person was or the more important the person was, the more care and more time they took mummifying the body.

Below are spaces for the steps that the Egypt gang followed in mummifying Pete-ho-tep. Some of them have been filled in. Use your book to identify each step in its correct order. There is a total of eight steps.

The Steps for the Funeral Ceremony and Preparation of the Dead

1. ______________________________
2. March around the altar wailing and mourning.
3. ______________________________
4. ______________________________
5. ______________________________
6. Anoint the body with spices and perfume.
7. ______________________________
8. ______________________________

Develop a Paragraph

On your own paper use the above list of steps to prepare a paragraph that explains how Pete-ho-tep was mummified. Write the explanation as a paragraph and remember to indent the first line. You may also add details that further explain each step.

Name______________________________ Date________________

The Egypt Game

The Oracle of Thoth/The Oracle Speaks

Before You Read

"What would you do if you had only one wish?" Everyone at one time or another has thought of that question or asked that question of someone else. The obvious answer, of course, is "I'd ask for more wishes." It's just a dream to imagine that a wish for anything in the world could come true just by asking. For many years, however, people have asked other equally impossible questions and expected (even believed in) the answer. These are questions about the future.

We would all like to look into the future and see what it holds for us. Will we be rich someday? Will we grow up to be something special? Will we get an "A" on a certain test? Wouldn't it be great to have a way of getting those answers?

So pretend for just a little while that there was a way of asking those questions and getting answers (perhaps a crystal ball or a wise old hermit). What would you *really* want to know? On the lines below list five questions about your future that you would want to know.

1. ______________________________
2. ______________________________
3. ______________________________
4. ______________________________
5. ______________________________

A Class Poll

If you have time, take a class survey of the one question about the future that each classmate would like answered. Do this by making a list of the questions and then recording how often certain questions are asked. Be prepared to report your results.

As You Read

In the next two chapters the Egypt gang gets involved in a very strange and very mysterious happening. They begin to ask questions of the Egyptian gods and have them answered. Read to find out how this comes about, what questions are asked and what answers they get. Look for clues that might help you to understand this mystery.

Name______________________________ Date______________

The Egypt Game

The Oracle of Thoth/The Oracle Speaks

After You Read

Memory Buster

After you've read this chapter and feel you understand it, close the book and see what you can recall about it from memory. Don't look in the book until you have answered as many questions as possible. When you are done, open your book and check the answers you've written. Put the page number where you find that answer in the space after the question. Fill in any missing answers.

1. How did the Egypt gang get the idea for an oracle? p. _____

   ____

2. What is an oracle? p. _____

   ____

3. Who came up with the first oracle plan? p. _____

   ____

4. Whose oracle plan did they use? p. _____

   ____

5. What object became the god Thoth and why? p. _____

   ____

6. According to the oracle ceremony, how was the question supposed to be answered? p. _____

   ____

7. Who got to ask the first question? p. _____

   ____

8. Who was in charge of the ceremony the next day? p. _____

   ____

9. Why did April stomp out of the temple when she read the paper? p. _____

   ____

10. What was Ken's question? p. _____

    ____

11. Everyone accused everyone else of writing the answer to the oracle. How was the argument settled? p. _____

    ____

Super Trivia Question

What was the response to Ken's question?

____

Name________________________________ Date________________

The Egypt Game

The Oracle of Thoth/The Oracle Speaks

After You Read

Step-by-Step

In developing the ceremony in which the question was answered by the oracle, the Egypt gang had to invent certain steps. On the lines below list the steps for the ceremony. A few steps have been done for you.

Ceremony for Answering the Question

1. Everyone made twisted paper logs to burn and lined up.
2. ________________________________
3. ________________________________
4. April lit the candles, incense and sacred fire and put the fire bowl on the floor before the altar of Thoth.
5. ________________________________
6. ________________________________
7. ________________________________
8. ________________________________
9. ________________________________
10. ________________________________

Toby also had a ceremony for asking the oracle a question, but it was not so elaborate. On the lines below, see if you can re-create the entire ceremony yourself. You could have five to eight steps.

Ceremony for Asking the Oracle a Question

1. ________________________________
2. ________________________________
3. ________________________________
4. ________________________________
5. ________________________________
6. ________________________________
7. ________________________________
8. ________________________________

Name______________________________________ Date___________________

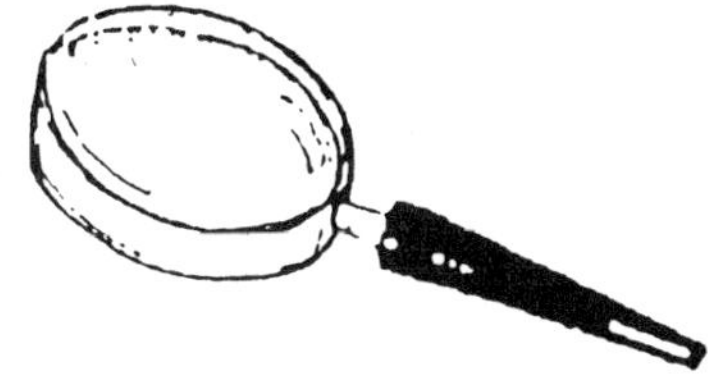

The Egypt Game

The Detective's Handbook

Who Done It?

Earlier in the story, a crime was committed but never solved. Up until now that crime has not been a major part of the plot. Now the Egypt gang has another mystery, and this one will prove to be very important. The mystery is who wrote the answer to Ken's question? To begin, as a detective you must make a simple decision. Was it really the god Thoth, or did someone else sneak in and answer the question?

A good detective does not just take a side and ignore everything else and neither will you. Begin by thinking about whether or not the question really could have been answered by Thoth. On the lines below list four to six reasons why it *could* have been Thoth.

______________________________ ______________________________

______________________________ ______________________________

______________________________ ______________________________

List four to six reasons why it *could not* have been Thoth.

______________________________ ______________________________

______________________________ ______________________________

______________________________ ______________________________

Another possibility is that someone is sneaking around and answering the question. For that we need *suspects*. A suspect is someone who you believe could have done it. To be a suspect, a person needs the *opportunity* or chance to do whatever it is you suspect him/her of doing. The person also needs a *motive* or reason for doing it.

For example, you could decide that Mr. Schmitt of Schmitt's Variety Store is a suspect. In considering him as a suspect, you would first have to decide if he had the opportunity to sneak in and write the message. The answer to that is "yes!" He could have gotten in when the children were in school and written it. Next, you must decide if he has a motive for doing it. Here you would have to answer "no." You have read nothing in the story so far that would give him the reason to try and trick the Egypt gang. In fact, he doesn't seem to care about children enough to bother with them. In the end, Mr. Schmitt does not make a very good suspect.

Your Turn

Use the Detective's Suspect Chart to come up with your best suspect.

Name____ Date____________________

The Egypt Game

Detective's Suspect Chart

In the boxes below list all the information you can for each suspect. Try to think like a detective who suspects everyone. Don't make up information, but don't overlook any either.

Name of Suspect	Did this person have opportunity? If "yes," when was it?	Did this person have a motive? If "yes," what is it?

The Final Decision

Now that you've worked out your suspects and analyzed their opportunities and motives, it's time to decide on your number one suspect. On your own paper write a paragraph in which you tell who your number one suspect is and why. If you don't have any suspect at all, maybe you will want to suspect Thoth.

Name________________________________ Date________________

The Egypt Game

Where Is Security?/Confession and Confusion

As You Read

Sometimes the most likely events and characters can lead to the solving of a mystery. In these two chapters that is exactly what happens. Read "Where Is Security?" to find out how Marshall forces the Egypt gang to find out who or what has been writing the notes. Then read "Confession and Confusion" in order to find how the mystery continues.

After You Read

Vocabulary

Slang Words

Words have a way of changing. They change when people decide to use them in a different way. The word *rat,* for example, usually means "a type of small rodent"; but in this book it was used to mean "the act of tattling on someone." When a word develops a special meaning in addition to its usual meaning, we call that word a slang word. Slang words come and go in our language. One generation of people will begin to use a word in a special way that other generations of people do not. Throughout the book, the girls and boys of the Egypt gang have been using slang words.

Below is a list of five slang words found in the two chapters you've just read. Begin by finding each one and putting its page number after it. Then match the slang word to its meaning by drawing a line between the word and its definition.

Slang Words	Meanings
1. cop out p. _____	to leave in a hurry
2. dig p. _____	to quit or give up
3. fish p. _____	to become insane
4. cut out p. _____	to look suspicious
5. crack up p. _____	to enjoy or like something

Below are some more slang words used in these two chapters. After each write the page number where you found it and your own definition.

1. wise guy p. _____ – ________________________________
2. blast p. _____ – ________________________________
3. clinch p. _____ – ________________________________
4. hocus-pocus p. _____ – ________________________________

Name______________________________________ Date__________________

The Egypt Game

Fact or Opinion

Was Toby really behind all the trickery? Is there something magical about the Egypt temple the children created? Who wrote the message that told Marshall where Security was? Things are getting confusing. What's your opinion on these questions?

An opinion is an idea a person believes but can't prove is true. An opinion might also be someone's feelings about something or his judgement. For example, Ken thought that the Egypt game was kind of crazy at first. That was his opinion. Toby thought the game was terrific. That, too, was his opinion. Opinions are sometimes easy to identify. For example, opinions sometimes have judgement words in them like *good* or *bad.* Also, anytime someone predicts what is going to happen, it is an opinion. Opinions can have words like *probably* or *maybe* in them.

A fact is quite different from an opinion. A fact is an idea that is true or can be proven true. A fact is something that is known for certain. For example, in the story we know that the statue of Thoth was made from an old stuffed owl. That is a fact, but be careful. Agreeing with an opinion does not make it a fact.

A reader of mysteries is always looking for facts. By getting the facts he/she can usually piece together a solution to the mystery. Below are ten statements. You must decide which ones are fact and which ones are opinion. Put the letter *F* in the space before the ones that are facts and the letter *O* in the space before the ones that are opinions.

1. _____ The professor probably is the murderer.
2. _____ April felt angry when she received bad news from Dorothea.
3. _____ Ken has a bad imagination.
4. _____ Toby avoids acting especially friendly toward girls in public.
5. _____ Ken was the first person to ask the oracle a question.
6. _____ The Egypt gang has managed to summon up real Egyptian gods.
7. _____ Toby is going to try to fool the Egypt gang again.
8. _____ The "land of Egypt" is being watched by someone who is not a member of the Egypt gang.
9. _____ The Egypt gang made their temple out of found objects.
10. _____ Ken is going to quit the Egypt game.

Name______________________________________ Date__________________

The Egypt Game

Fear Strikes/The Hero

Before You Read

Suspense

One of the elements of a mystery is suspense. Suspense is the feeling of excitement you get when you want to know what is going to happen next in the story. A story like *The Egypt Game* is suspenseful because you want to solve the mystery.

There have been two mysteries in the story so far. The first one happened early in the story but has not been a big part of the chapters lately. The second mystery involves the Egypt game itself and the messages. Write what you think the two mysteries of this story are on the lines below.

1. ____
2. ____

Suspense has been building up gradually ever since the girls and Marshall discovered Egypt. In fact, there have been several suspenseful moments. For example, one of the suspenseful moments was when the girls went to the land of Egypt on Halloween and were surprised and scared by the boys as they jumped over the fence into the middle of the yard.

On the lines below list two more suspenseful moments from the story.

1. ____
2. ____

Another way suspense can be built is with a suspenseful setting. Most of the story takes place in the storage yard behind the professor's store where the Egypt game is played. At different times, though, that setting can seem more mysterious than others. On the lines below list two times in the story when the land of Egypt was especially mysterious. Include the page number where you found it and be prepared to read the mysterious or suspenseful description that you found.

1. p. _____ – ______________________________________

____

2. p. _____ – ______________________________________

____

As You Read

Both mysteries of this book are about to come together. The suspense is strongest in these two chapters. Read to find out the terrible thing that happens to April when she realizes her math book has been left in Egypt. Notice the suspenseful setting and all the suspenseful moments.

Name____ Date____________________

The Egypt Game

Fear Strikes/The Hero

After You Read

Cause and Effect

In a good mystery all the events build on each other. One event leads to or causes another. Review the entire story by completing the sentences below. Write what should come after the word *because*.

Example: Toby and Ken found out about the Egypt game *because*

they followed the Egypt gang to the storage yard on Halloween night.

1. Toby and Ken were willing to keep the Egypt game a secret *because*

____

2. When a secret message written by one of the Egypt gang was found in school, no one could guess what it said or whose it was *because*

____

3. The Egypt gang was able to create a ceremony for the dead *because*

____

4. Toby insisted that the questions not be written in hieroglyphics, and he insisted that everyone bow low when he placed the question in the owl's mouth *because*

____

5. Toby tried especially hard to talk Marshall out of asking a question, and he was especially worried when Marshall did anyway *because*

____

6. April returned to Egypt at night with Marshall *because*

____

7. Marshall knew that the professor might be watching that night and shined the light on the professor's back window *because*

____

8. Mr. Schmitt may have tried to get people stirred up against the professor after the first murder *because*

____

Name______________________________ Date________________

The Egypt Game

Gains and Losses/Christmas Keys

As You Read

The action of the story seems to be over, but there are still some loose ends that need to be tied up. For example, how did the professor know to look out the window that night? What will happen with April and her mother Dorothea? Is the Egypt game over now that everyone knows what has been going on? Read to find out the answers to these and other questions you may have.

After You Read

Tieing Up Loose Ends

On the lines below answer each of the questions which has to do with all the details of the story. Be ready to share your answers and show where you found them in the chapter.

1. How were the neighborhood people able to show the professor that they were sorry for wrongly accusing him?

   ____

   ____

2. Did Dorothea ever ask April to come live with her?

   ____

   ____

3. How do we know that April has come to accept Caroline as a grandmother?

   ____

   ____

4. Why is it that the professor happened to be looking out his back window when April was attacked?

   ____

   ____

5. What arrangements have been made to allow the children to continue the Egypt game or any game they wish in the storage yard?

   ____

   ____

Name________________________________ Date__________________

The Egypt Game

Gains and Losses/Christmas Keys

Predicting

All's well that ends well. The kids have keys to the storage area; the professor has a booming business; April and Caroline are getting along fine and April seems to no longer resent her mother. Even Mrs. Chung got a job out of the whole adventure.

Wouldn't it be interesting to see what was happening to these characters in seven years' time? That would make April and Melanie eighteen years old, Elizabeth sixteen years old and Marshall eleven years old.

On the lines below write a few brief lines telling what will be happening in each character's life in seven years. Try to think about each character's personality and interests in coming up with your answers.

April ____

____

Melanie ____

____

Elizabeth ____

____

Dorothea ____

____

The Professor ____

____

Toby ____

____

Ken ____

____

Supplemental Vocabulary

Not all the lessons contain vocabulary work. Nonetheless, you may want to supplement your teaching with additional vocabulary work from time to time. Below are additional lists of words by chapters. No more than seven words per chapter are included. Chapters that have lessons with vocabulary work have been excluded.

The Discovery of Egypt
1. curios
2. trace
3. gunnysack
4. lean-to
5. pert
6. ornate
7. improvised

Enter April
1. righteous
2. prim
3. facade
4. dingy
5. treadle
6. cultivated
7. notion

Enter Melanie and Marshall
1. tenants
2. warily
3. vocalist
4. haughty
5. caper
6. escapades
7. content

Eyelashes and Ceremony
1. triumphant
2. treacherous
3. leer
4. brooded
5. mystic
6. bust
7. sinister

Neferbeth
1. ambushed
2. pang
3. enchanted
4. touchy
5. profile

Prisoners of Fear
1. languishing
2. clamored
3. remedial
4. medley
5. persistent
6. splendors
7. sheer

Summoned by the Mighty Ones
1. chaperoned
2. downright
3. raptly
4. monolith
5. quavered
6. token
7. omen

The Return to Egypt
1. milling
2. exasperated
3. momentum
4. swagger
5. convulsions
6. prostrate

Moods and Maybes
1. spring
2. restricted
3. devastated
4. reluctant
5. scrolls
6. rituals

Hieroglyphics
1. well-preserved
2. balefully
3. intriguing
4. deciphered
5. borders
6. fluent

The Oracle of Thoth
1. oracle
2. grotto
3. vapors
4. trance
5. scheme
6. consternation
7. solemnity

The Oracle Speaks
1. prearrangement
2. pilgrimage
3. fasting
4. regal
5. accusation
6. staggering
7. presided

Fear Strikes
1. gloat
2. fuming
3. lurk
4. steadfastly
5. drone

The Hero
1. mussed
2. vividly
3. soothingly
4. suspect
5. bewildered
6. alibi
7. unjustly

Gains and Losses
1. lair
2. seclusion
3. browsers
4. gravelly
5. grave
6. verge
7. sequins

Christmas Keys
1. speculated
2. anthropology
3. optimistic
4. mission
5. intent
6. plead
7. pried

Extension Activities

Picture It

The setting of this story appears to be within the confines of a city. All the main characters live in the Casa Rosada; "Egypt" is behind the A-Z Curios and Antique Shop; Mr. Schmitt's variety store is nearby as are a doughnut shop, florist and a drugstore. Billboards and alleyways are also included. Have students diagram the layout of this urban neighborhood. For accuracy, have them reread the first two chapters and list all the different shops and stores mentioned as well as their relative locations. A lesson labeling and titling diagrams would fit here nicely. If they want, they could also color code or number the houses and key them at the bottom.

If the students have had perspective lessons in art, they may be able to draw the street with its buildings and store fronts. Orchard Avenue would be the street that grows smaller toward the vanishing point with the various apartments and stores on each side of the street.

As preparation or follow-up, students could also diagram their own neighborhoods. A listing of similarities and differences could then be developed between theirs and the story's neighborhood with a discussion or writing assignment as additional follow-up. It would be interesting for students who do not live in a city to imagine what it is like to walk no more than a block and have so much available.

Cultures

In the story, Orchard Avenue is presented as a street with people from every conceivable continent and culture. Certainly the main characters of the story provide a basis to believe that. An interesting poll for the students to take would be to have them find out all the different nationalities found within their own classroom. The poll can be as detailed or simplified as you wish, depending on how you want them to record people with several nationalities in their backgrounds. If you have many students reading the book, the survey can be extended to include other classrooms. Lessons on developing surveys and recording the data would be needed to set the activity up. Follow-up math activities could include lessons on percentages in order to figure percentages of certain racial or ethnic groups.

You could also follow up with activities on graphing with students designing bar graphs to show their results.

If you're studying American history, this would be a good time to mention the waves of immigration that took place in America during the 1830's and 1840's as well as at the turn of the century and again after World War II.

Chapter Titles and Illustrations: See page 162.

Acrostic Poems: See page 38.

Slang Study

Included in the lessons on page 71 is a lesson dealing with slang vocabulary. Slang of the 1960's and 1970's is sprinkled throughout the book. Have students create a slang dictionary for the entire book using slang terms they find from chapter to chapter. This can be introduced early and then developed throughout the reading of the entire story.

As a follow-up, they can then create their own slang dictionary of the 1990's. This would include slang (not vulgarities) of their generation. Still another idea is to have them interview grandparents to get slang from yet another generation. This activity is great to have students see how language constantly changes while reinforcing dictionary skills.

Ceremonies

The Egypt gang did a terrific job integrating their research about ancient Egypt into their ceremonies. Have students re-create any of the ceremonies described in the story. The step-by-step procedures can be found in the "Ceremonies for the Dead" and "The Oracle of Thoth." If anything seems to be missing from the ceremony, the students can fill in the missing steps.

Another extension would be to have students report on other ceremonies that are a part of their religion or culture. This could include funerary ceremonies, cultural celebrations in the home of religious events such as Hanukkah, Ramadan, Christmas, etc.

Depending on the student with whom you are working, another very interesting study is to examine ceremonies that different cultures have developed for the dead.

Point of View

The story is seen almost entirely from the view point of the children. Nonetheless, we learn the professor has been watching every day. Have one or several students retell part of the story from the professor's point of view. How would he explain the goings-on? Would he compliment them on their authenticity? Would he be critical of their foolishness to come out late at night? What would he have to say about the way people treated him after the first child was killed? This activity could be done with any character, even the children, as long as a specific scene is identified for them to discuss.

News Article/Interview

Following the attack on April, newspaper and media must have swarmed the neighborhood. Have students act out an on-the-spot interview for an imaginary news channel. Students can take the roles of April, Marshall, the professor, police chief, Mr. Schmitt, newscaster, etc. They would need to prepare for this by writing questions and answers and rehearsing before putting it on for the class.

A variation of this is to set it up as a talk show. An Oprah or Phil Donahue type setting could be designed with audience members (classmates) actually taking part in the questions.

Hieroglyphics

The Egypt gang created a hieroglyphic alphabet that was so good that no one at Wilson School could figure out what their secret message said when it was passed around. Hieroglyphic writing is nothing more than picture writing. In ancient Egypt each picture stood for an idea, event or person. Consequently thousands of pictures were needed to tell a story.

A hieroglyphic alphabet is different. All that is needed are twenty-six pictures to represent the twenty-six letters of the alphabet. Students will enjoy inventing their own hieroglyphic alphabet. Lots of possibilities are available. Each picture could be an object that begins with the letter of the alphabet being represented. On the other hand, it could end with the letter of the alphabet being represented. If a key is kept by the student, then there doesn't have to be any relationship between picture and letter.

Each student can also decide on his own picture to represent his name. An interesting discussion/writing could follow in which students compare and contrast picture writing with our traditional alphabet noticing the flexibility and ease of our own alphabet in comparison to hieroglyphics.

Still another offshoot of this activity is to have students investigate their alphabets including ancient ones such as cuneiform writing of ancient Mesopotamia, the current Russian, Oriental or Native American alphabets (specifically the Navajo have coded their language).

Finally, they may want to invent their own coded language with numbers or geometric symbols representing the alphabet letters.

Oracles

Ancient oracles were shrines consecrated to the consultation of a prophetic god. The actual prophecies were called oracles, too. Oracles, however, are not the only way people have tried to learn of the future. Through the ages, dozens of methods have been used. Students may find it interesting to investigate some of these including rune casting as practiced by many northern European cultures in the first millenium AD, astrology, palmistry and even phrenology (reading the bumps on one's head).

Costumes

The Egypt gang designed and wore some interesting Egyptian costumes. They were also very resourceful in creating them. Have students design their own Egyptian costumes to wear to class one day. Insist that they be made out of found objects. They do not need to develop a complete outfit, only design one item to wear.

Research and Report

Many topics for research evolve out of this story including:

- The Life and Times of Ancient Egypt (dress, religion, transportation, ceremonies, foods, government, living quarters)
- The Life and Times of Some Other Ancient Culture
- Egyptian Gods and Goddesses
- Greek and Roman Gods and Goddesses (for comparison)

Reader's Theater: See page 37.

The Curse of the Blue Figurine

by

John Bellairs

When Johnny Dixon's mother dies and his father is asked to serve in the Korean War, Johnny has to go and live with his grandparents in Duston Heights, Massachusetts. Johnny is a bright boy full of imagination who doesn't mind reading and loves to listen to scary radio programs. One January night just after dinner, they are visited by Professor Roderick Childermass who tells them the story of Father Remigius Baart who was the rector in the 1880's of the local parish. According to the story, Father Baart began acting in a dastardly way after being visited by a traveling wood-carver. Several of the parishioners who openly criticized Father Baart died under mysterious circumstances. Soon afterward, Father Baart disappeared leaving only an obscure message. Johnny with his keen imagination wants to believe the legend, but even the professor admits most of it is hearsay.

Several days later Johnny enters the church's basement to escape the local bully. While he is there he finds a hollowed-out book with a blue figurine and scroll. The writing on the scroll is a warning not to remove either item from the church. As luck would have it, however, Johnny hears someone coming and dashes out of the basement with materials still in his clutches.

Johnny shows the figurine to the professor who admits that the writing is Father Baart's but disappointingly finds proof that the thing is a hoax. Mysteriously, however, strange things begin happening to the house and Johnny. Feeling confused and scared, Johnny goes to the church to pray. While he is there he meets a friendly stranger who gives him some advice and a ring. The ring gives Johnny strange powers which scare him. Slowly, Johnny becomes a wreck, physically and emotionally. When he tries to give the ring back to the stranger, he finds out that this man is really Father Baart's ghost who intends to take Johnny for disobeying the warning. No one can see this ghost but Johnny. Consequently, both grandparents and the professor think he has developed a mental problem related to the loss of his mother and father.

When school lets out, the professor takes Johnny on a vacation in order to help relieve the stress he imagines Johnny is feeling. The ghost follows them, and in a climactic finish, almost succeeds in getting Johnny. Luckily, the open-minded professor learns of what is happening and manages to save Johnny at the last minute.

Note to the Teacher:
This book has been so well received by my students that they have literally begged me to bring more of John Bellairs' books in for reading. This was especially evident among students who rarely read books on their own but who have now finished many of this author's books independently.

Name______________________________ Date______________

Chapter 1: The Curse of the Blue Figurine

Before You Read

Around Halloween everyone likes to tell or hear a good ghost story. Storytelling can be exciting for the teller as well as the listener. We've all heard certain ghost stories. We tell them ourselves. We change them, make them better and even create new ones.

Before you begin reading *The Curse of the Blue Figurine,* plan on telling a ghost story. It can be a story you've heard before, one that you've read, even one that you made up yourself. Just for fun plan on starting your story in the way hundreds of the best mystery stories have started, with the words *It was a dark and stormy night....* On the lines below outline your story idea. You don't need to write down everything you are going to say. Write down the basic story line so that you can remember how the story goes.

____

____

____

____

____

____

____

____

____

____

____

____

____

Now practice telling your story with a buddy. Tell it several times and even talk with your buddy about what can be added to the story to make it better. Be ready to tell your story by ______________________.

Name______________________________________ Date____________________

Chapter 1: The Curse of the Blue Figurine

As You Read

The first chapter of a book is usually important because the author has so many things to introduce. He wants to introduce the characters of the story (at least the main ones). He also wants to create a setting for the story. Finally, he wants to get the plot of the story underway, and in a mystery he wants to introduce some of the mysterious elements.

Setting, character and plot are all described in more detail below and on the following pages. As you read Chapter 1, see if you can identify all three.

Setting

The setting of a story is where and when a story takes place. The setting may change from chapter to chapter and may even change within a chapter, but usually the overall setting of a mystery remains the same in a story.

John Bellairs has made it easy to figure out the setting of this story because he comes right out and tells you. Read closely.

1. In what year does the story take place? ______________________________
2. In what season does the story begin? ______________________________
3. Where in the United States does the story take place?______________________________
4. Exactly where does the action take place in Chapter 1? ______________________________

Name_______________________________________ Date____________________

Chapter 1: The Curse of the Blue Figurine

Characters

The characters of the story are the people in the story. Sometimes the characters are not human being-type people. They can sometimes be ghosts, spirits or even animals. You may remember reading stories in which animals were the characters of the story. In this story, however, the characters are mostly regular human beings.

1. On the lines below list all the characters that are actually present in the first chapter.

    ______________________________ ______________________________

    ______________________________ ______________________________

2. Now list six characters that are mentioned but not actually present in the first chapter. You don't need to include the book authors that are mentioned.

    ______________________________ ______________________________

    ______________________________ ______________________________

    ______________________________ ______________________________

Some of these characters will become main characters of the story. You may or may not be able to tell which ones. Put a star by the ones on either list that you think will become main characters of this story.

Name____________________________________ Date__________________

Chapter 1: The Curse of the Blue Figurine

Plot: What Happened?

The plot of a story is what happens in the story. It is the action of the story. In the case of Chapter 1 it includes not only what happened but also the story that Professor Childermass told. All of it is part of the plot.

To make sure that you caught some of the important events of Chapter 1, answer the questions below.

1. Why is Johnny not living with his parents? ______________________________

   ____

2. How did Johnny and Grandpa help the professor? __________________________

   ____

3. What is Johnny's latest interest? ______________________________________

   ____

4. According to the professor's story, who did Father Baart meet that changed his life?

   ____

5. List two strange things that happened to people in Father Baart's parish.

   a. ____

   b. ____

6. Whatever happened to Father Baart?_______________________________________

   ____

Name________________________________ Date________________

Chapter 2: The Curse of the Blue Figurine

Before You Read

Any good mystery is built on clues. A clue is a piece of information that guides you to the solution of the mystery. It is still a little early in the story to be getting clues to a solution. However, we have begun to get clues to what the mystery will involve. Here are a few.

1. Johnny is interested in ancient Egyptian archaeology.
2. Father Baart hires a mysterious wood-carver named Nemo.
3. Father Baart's behavior changes after supposedly taking a gift from the wood-carver.

See if you can add to this list with two or three of your own.

1. ____

____

2. ____

____

3. ____

____

It would probably be a good idea to go back and reread the story that Professor Childermass tells Johnny. All the details of the story will be important later on.

As You Read

In the first chapter all the main characters are introduced. In the second chapter the plot gets underway. Remember that the plot is the action of the story. All good plots are based on problems that the main character has to solve.

Read Chapter 2. As you read this chapter, pay attention to what problem Johnny has and how it leads him deeper into the mystery.

Name____ Date____________________

Chapter 2: The Curse of the Blue Figurine

After You Read

Vocabulary

Context Clues

Sometimes words have different definitions, and when you go to look them up in the dictionary, you don't know which one to use. In order to select the right definition, you need to look at the way the word was used in the sentence and match the most likely definition with the way it is used.

The words below are all found in Chapter 2. After each one are two likely definitions for the word. Only one is the definition that fits the story. Use your book to locate the word, see how it is used in the sentence and select the correct definition. Circle the letter of the correct definition. The words are listed in the order you would find them in the chapter.

scapulars: A. feathers covering the shoulders of a bird
B. a sleeveless outer garment hanging from the shoulders

vestibule: A. an enclosed area at the end of a passenger car
B. a small entrance hall between two doors; a lobby

pew: A. a long bench on which people sit
B. a strong odor

incense: A. praise or admiration
B. a substance that burns with a pleasant odor

sanctuary: A. the most holy part of a church or temple
B. any place of safety for animals or people

niches: A. a cutout area of a wall for holding a statue
B. an activity that is suited for a person's talents

censer: A. a vessel that holds incense
B. a person who examines films or books in order to decide whether other people should see them

belfry: A. the basement of a church
B. a tower or steeple in which one or more bells are hung

missal: A. any prayer book
B. an object or weapon that is thrown or fired

crook: A. one who dishonestly takes from other people
B. an object with a bent or curved part

Name______________________________ Date______________

Creating a Mood

In a mystery, authors like to create a certain mood with the action. Usually that mood is one of suspense, fear, horror, eeriness or suspicion. John Bellairs has done a nice job of just that. What type of moods have been created in the story so far? Use the lines below for your answer.

One of the moods that was created was ______________________________.

Some of the action that helped create this mood includes ______________________

The author can also help create the mood with the setting he chooses. What setting in Chapter 2 was particularly creepy?

On the lines below copy some of the sentences from Chapter 2 that describe the creepy setting.

Finally, circle any of the words you copied that really help create that creepy mood.

Name______________________________________ Date__________________

Chapter 3: The Curse of the Blue Figurine

Productive Thinking

The professor has some interesting words taped to the inside of his fuss closet. If you've forgotten them, go back and look.

Like everyone, the professor gets frustrated, aggravated and just plain angry at things from time to time. But, unlike so many of us, the professor has found a way of taking out his anger. He just goes into his fuss closet and pounds, kicks, yells and in general throws a temper tantrum without anyone getting in the way.

That's pretty smart of the professor. We all need a way to blow off some steam from time to time.

Certainly there are other ways of letting off anger besides creating a fuss closet. That's what your job is going to be. You are to come up with many different and unusual ways a person could release his/her anger without hurting or bothering someone else. The idea is to come up with as many as you can!

When you are done, choose your best one and explain why it would be so effective at releasing the anger and tension a person would feel. Use the Productive Thinking Work Sheet to help you organize your ideas.

Name________________________ Date______________

Productive Thinking Work Sheet

Part One

On the lines below list the many different and unusual ways you could release tension and anger without hurting or bothering someone. Do not try to explain them in detail. Use a few words to describe them. If you need more space, use your own paper.

1. ______________________
2. ______________________
3. ______________________
4. ______________________
5. ______________________
6. ______________________
7. ______________________
8. ______________________
9. ______________________
10. ______________________

Now look over your list and select the best two and copy them on the lines below.

My Two Best Ideas

1. ______________________
2. ______________________

Now that you've narrowed down your decision, you have to pick one from these two. Think about each one and decide which is your best idea. Once you have done that, write a paragraph that does two things.

First, describe this anger-releasing method in detail. If it involves building something, explain what it should look like. If it involves following a set of steps, describe each step in detail.

When you are done, explain why you think this method would be so good at releasing anger.

Name______________________________ Date______________

Chapter 3: The Curse of the Blue Figurine

After You Read
Vocabulary

Slang Words

A slang word is a word that is not used in a way that matches its regular definition. For example, if a character in a story says that a car is really cool, he wouldn't mean that the car has a low temperature. What he would mean is that the car is really nice looking. The word *cool* is the slang word in that sentence.

All the words listed below are slang words from Chapter 3. You may or may not find their slang definitions in the dictionary. Consequently, you will need to figure some of them out yourself. Go back to the story and reread the sentences where these words are found. Use the clues you get in the sentence to figure out what they mean.

waltzing: ______________________________

____

nutty: ______________________________

____

harrumphed: ______________________________

____

drag: ______________________________

____

Name________________________________ Date____________________

Chapter 3: The Curse of the Blue Figurine

Before You Read

A good reader is always thinking ahead. In this story Johnny has stumbled upon a very mysterious object and message. Not only is it mysterious, but it is also threatening! Think for a minute, what would you do if you were Johnny . . . the adventurous thing which is to take the book and its objects . . . or the safe thing which is to return it to its original place? Remember, there are consequences for whatever decision you make. Once you've decided, write your answer in the space below and go on to the next section. But be careful.

____

As You Read

Do you know what a souvenir is? It is something you get from a place you've visited to help you remember that place. The book Johnny will take from the basement of the church certainly is a souvenir, but read to find out how it is more than just a souvenir of Johnny's little adventure.

Name________________________________ Date________________

Chapter 3: The Curse of the Blue Figurine

Before You Read

Darn! Just when you think you've got a good mystery going, the mystery turns out to be something logical and normal. Isn't that the way it always is? Well maybe not. Good mystery writers purposely lead their readers to believe one thing so that they can surprise them with something else.

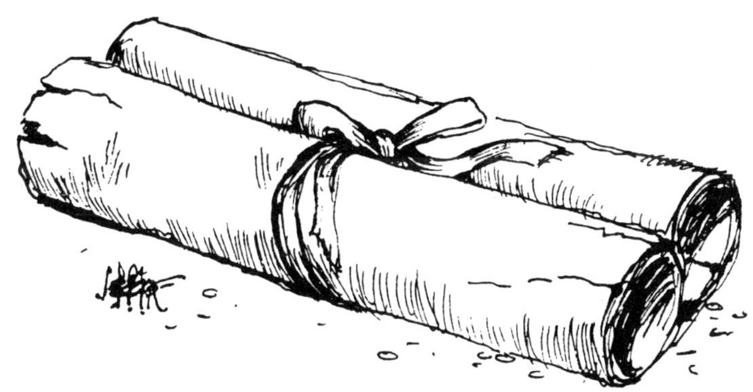

Good mystery readers know this and are always on the lookout for clues. Before you read this chapter, review the clues from the last chapter that led you to believe the statue and the scroll belonged to Father Baart. List those clues below. You do not have to fill up all the spaces, but you should come up with at least three clues.

1. ______________________________
2. ______________________________
3. ______________________________
4. ______________________________
5. ______________________________
6. ______________________________

As You Read

Since you are a good mystery reader, you must now be on the lookout for clues. As you read this chapter try to pick out clues that would lead you to believe that the statue and scroll are more than just a souvenir of Cairo.

Name________________________________ Date________________

Chapter 4: The Curse of the Blue Figurine

After You Read

Vocabulary

More Slang Words

Some slang is more than just one word. Sometimes it is a whole phrase. Other slang words are not even words you've seen before. See if you can figure out what these slang words and phrases from Chapter 4 mean.

hangdog, guilty look ________________________________

____

pull the rug out from under you________________________________

____

doojigger________________________________

____

doohickey ________________________________

____

Memory Buster

Are you following the story? Let's see what you remember. With your book closed, answer these questions that refer to Chapters 3 and 4. Answer as many as you can. When you are done, you can open your book and check the answers you've written and try to find the answers you missed. Put the page number where you found the correct answer in the space next to the question.

1. What caused Johnny to leave the church with the book? p. _____

   ____

2. What was the professor doing when Johnny came to talk to him? p. _____

   ____

3. What conclusion did the professor draw about the statue, and what led him to that conclusion? p. _____

   ____

4. How were ancient Egyptian ushabtis used? p. _____

   ____

5. What did the professor suggest Johnny do with his souvenir? p. _____

____

6. What did Johnny see as he left the professor's that night? p. _____

____

Super Trivia Question

The professor said his area of specialty is not the study of ancient Egypt. What is the professor's area of specialty? p. _____

____

Clues

The first job when you're reading a mystery is actually the toughest. It is to identify the clues. The second job which can be a little easier is to sort them out.

Below is a list of clues that you need to sort. Some of them lead us to believe that the book, statue and scroll are part of a mystery. Some of them lead us to believe that they are nothing but phony souvenirs.

You decide which is which. Put an *M* before the clues that lead us to believe that the things Johnny found are part of a *mystery*. Put an *S* before the clues that lead us to believe that the things Johnny found are just phony *souvenirs*.

1. __M__ spiders crawling on the book then disappearing suddenly
2. __S__ a small spider hole behind the bookcase
3. _____ The ribbon and scroll are very old.
4. _____ The writing is in Father Baart's handwriting.
5. _____ The label on the bottom of the statue is old.
6. _____ The label says the statue is from Cairo, Illinois.
7. _____ The professor likes to tell stories.
8. _____ Part of the professor's story did actually happen.
9. _____ Johnny's hands are always dirty after handling the book.
10. _____ When Johnny leaves the professor's house, someone is watching him.

Can you find any more clues for either side?

Name______________________________ Date________________

Chapter 5: The Curse of the Blue Figurine

Before You Read

In the pages you are about to read, Johnny is going to have an encounter with Eddie Tompke. Eddie is a bully. Do you know what a bully is? He is a person who uses his power to control others. His power might be physical power which means that he is bigger and stronger than the other person. Or his power might be that he has more authority than another person which means that he might be the person's boss.

Bullies are hard to deal with. Below write a paragraph in which you explain how a person can deal with a bully. In the paragraph mention two or three different ways and then tell which way is the best way and why.

____

____

____

____

____

____

____

____

____

____

____

____

____

As You Read

Johnny does not have much success dealing with Eddie Tompke in this chapter. Both boys end up hating each other. As you read this chapter focus your attention on what each boy does to show his hatred. What does Eddie do to Johnny; what does Johnny do to Eddie?

Name______________________________ Date__________________

Chapter 5: The Curse of the Blue Figurine

After You Read

There are several ways to figure out the meaning of a word. You can look for clues to the meaning of the word in the sentence or paragraph, or you can break the word down into its parts and figure it out. For the words below write a definition for each by using the method explained in the directions.

Context Clues

Use clues that you find in the sentence or paragraph to figure out your own definition of the word. Check your definition by looking the word up in the dictionary when you are done.

weary: ____

____

trouper: ____

____

severely: ____

____

Word Parts

Figure out your own definition of each word by breaking it down into parts or a base word.

scatterbrained: ____

____

apologetic: ____

____

hog-wild: ____

____

Apostrophes

You'll remember that an apostrophe takes the place of a letter or group of letters in a word. Look at these words found in Chapter 5. Next to each one write the full word without the apostrophe. The first one is done for you.

1. "'Smatter" = What's the matter?
2. "lyin'" = ____________________
3. "lotta" = ____________________
4. "'em" = ____________________
5. "'round" = ____________________
6. "'o" = ____________________

Name____ 

Chapter 5: The Curse of the Blue Figurine

Cause and Effect

"One thing always seems to lead to another." You may have heard someone say that at one time or maybe you've said it yourself. It is a true statement. One thing usually does lead to another. In fact one thing often causes another thing to happen. That's the way it has been in this story so far.

Johnny heard about Father Baart *because* he and Grandpa were nice enough to help the professor out of the snowdrift. Imagine how the story would have been different if they had simply refused to help the professor.

Below are several cause and effect sentences as they relate to Chapter 5. Read the beginning of each sentence and finish it by writing what should come after the word *because.*

Example: Johnny heard about the story of Father Baart *because*

he and Grandpa helped the professor and invited him in afterward.

1. Gramma was all upset one day in March *because*

____

2. The spiders and Johnny's dream have him worried *because*

____

3. Johnny goes to see the professor *because*

____

4. Johnny is working late after school *because*

____

5. Johnny goes to Sister Coreda's room *because*

____

6. Eddie gets mad when Johnny walks in on him *because*

____

7. Eddie hurt Johnny with the scissors *because*

____

8. That evening when Johnny is holding the figurine he gets scared *because*

____

Name____ Date____________________

Chapter 6: The Curse of the Blue Figurine

Before You Read

Have you ever felt rotten about yourself? Maybe you felt guilty for something you did to someone else, or maybe you felt bad because you failed to do something you were supposed to do. There are a lot of reasons for being upset with yourself and depressed. There are also a lot of ways of getting yourself to feel better. Below list ten ways you can make yourself feel better when you are depressed. Put a check by your two favorite ways.

1. ______________________________
2. ______________________________
3. ______________________________
4. ______________________________
5. ______________________________
6. ______________________________
7. ______________________________
8. ______________________________
9. ______________________________
10. ______________________________

As You Read

This chapter is a real shocker for Johnny. He begins to find out he has more power than he thought...or is it just his imagination? Well that's something you'll have to figure out. Read this chapter to find out what happened to Eddie Tompke and what Johnny did to make himself feel better.

Name_________________________________ Date_________________

Chapter 6: The Curse of the Blue Figurine

After You Read

Memory Buster

After you've read this chapter once, close the book and see what you can recall about it from memory. Don't look in the book until you have answers to as many questions as possible. When you are done, open your book, check the answers you've written and try to find the answers you've missed. Put the page number where you found the correct answer in the space next to the question.

1. What did Johnny find out happened to Eddie Tompke when he went to Mass the next morning? p. _____

   ____

2. Deep down inside, what does Johnny think caused Eddie's injury? p. _____

   ____

3. Johnny went to church that night but that isn't where he planned to go. Where did Johnny intend to go that evening before he changed his mind? p. _____

   ____

4. Johnny meets a stranger. What is the stranger's name? p. _____

   ____

5. Johnny tells the man everything about Eddie and the figurine. The man listens and gives him some advice. What was the advice? p. _____

   ____

6. The man also gives Johnny a ring. Where does he say he got it? p. _____

   ____

7. How does Johnny feel after his encounter with the man? p. _____

   ____

Super Trivia Question

Johnny entered the church and looked around; then he said a prayer. What was the next thing that he did?

____

Name________________________________ Date________________

The Curse of the Blue Figurine

Sequencing

The story is just about halfway over, and it has begun to get a bit complicated. So before you get into the second half of the book, review everything that has happened so far.

Below are ten sentences from the story you are reading. Put them in the order in which they happened by writing a 1 in front of the sentence that tells what happened first, a 2 in front of the sentence that tells what happened second and so on. Do this with the book closed and put your answers in the first set of spaces. Then check your answers and make any changes in the order in the second set of spaces.

_____ _____ Johnny is bullied by Eddie Tompke and curses him while holding the blue figurine.

_____ _____ The professor tells Johnny about Father Baart.

_____ _____ Johnny meets a stranger named Robert Beard who gives him a ring and some advice about how to make himself feel better.

_____ _____ Johnny begins having weird dreams and funny feelings, and spiders infest his home.

_____ _____ Johnny's mother dies and his dad goes off to war.

_____ _____ Johnny tells his grandparents he is going to the professor's house but goes to St. Michael's church instead.

_____ _____ Johnny finds the blue figurine and scroll while in the church basement.

_____ _____ The professor discovers a label on the figurine that says it is a souvenir of Cairo, Illinois.

_____ _____ Johnny and Grandpa help Professor Childermass out of a snowbank.

_____ _____ Johnny finds Eddie has broken his arm.

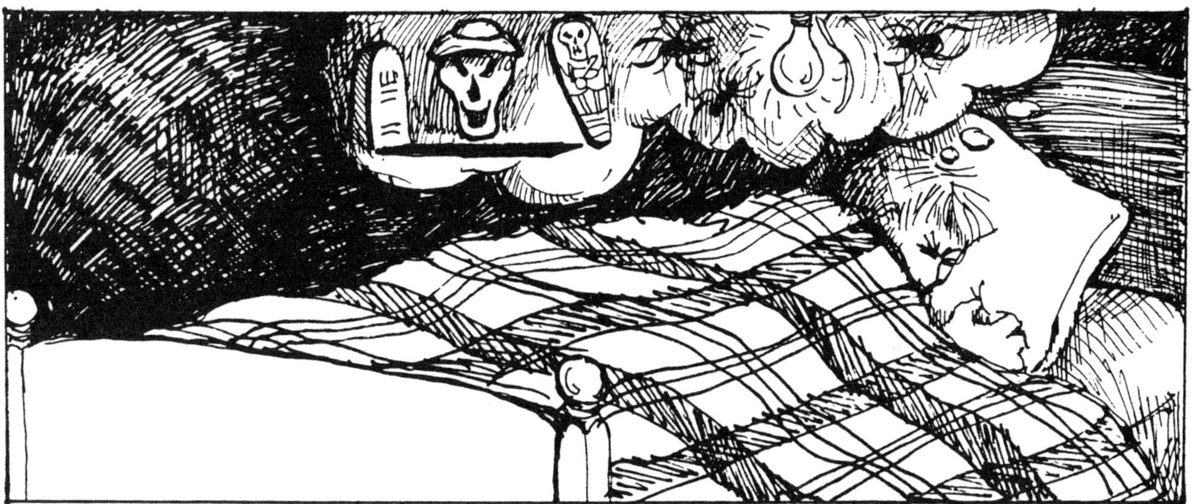

Name________________________________ Date________________

Chapter 7: The Curse of the Blue Figurine

Before You Read

In Chapter 5 Johnny had a dream, although it was closer to a nightmare. In Chapter 7 he has another nightmare. This one is similar to the one he had in Chapter 5 but changes a little. It isn't so unusual to have dreams that happen over and over again. Maybe you've even had one like that.

Before you read Chapter 7, recall a dream that you've had. Perhaps you can remember one that you've had more than once. If not, try to remember a recent one. Usually you can remember a little of it even if you can't remember the details.

On the lines below write down as much as you can remember about the dream. Then be prepared to share your dream story.

____

____

____

____

____

____

____

____

____

____

____

____

____

____

____

As You Read

In addition to our nighttime dreams, we often have daydreams as well. Johnny probably often daydreamed that he would have the power to put Eddie Tompke in his place. In this chapter Johnny starts to play a game that might lead to just that.

Read Chapter 7 in order to find out what game Johnny begins to play and what happens between Eddie and him.

Name_______________________________________ Date____________________

Chapter 7: The Curse of the Blue Figurine

Before You Read
Vocabulary

Base Words

A base word is a word to which a beginning (prefix) or an ending (suffix) has been added. Sometimes if you do not know the meaning of a word that has a suffix or prefix added to it, you can figure it out by first figuring out what the base word is.

Example: Professor Childermass said he was not an *Egyptologist*. You may not know what an Egyptologist is, but if you knew the base word was *Egypt*, you could probably figure out that any Egyptologist is someone who studies ancient Egypt.

With this in mind, write the base word for each of the words listed below that are in Chapter 7. Remember that the spelling of the base word may change when a prefix or suffix is added. Use a dictionary to check your work.

1. swiveling ____________________
2. figurine ____________________
3. grumblingly ____________________
4. moodily ____________________
5. accusingly ____________________
6. triumphant ____________________
7. irresistible ____________________
8. bedstead ____________________
9. processions ____________________
10. terrorize ____________________
11. accusations ____________________
12. unamused ____________________
13. monotone ____________________

Now see if you can find your own. Look through Chapter 7 and find five more words that have prefixes or suffixes added to them. List them below in the first column of spaces. Opposite each one list its base word. In the last small space list the page number where you found it.

	Word	Base Word	Page
1.	____________________	____________________	_____
2.	____________________	____________________	_____
3.	____________________	____________________	_____
4.	____________________	____________________	_____
5.	____________________	____________________	_____

Name______________________________________ Date____________________

The Curse of the Blue Figurine

Fact or Opinion

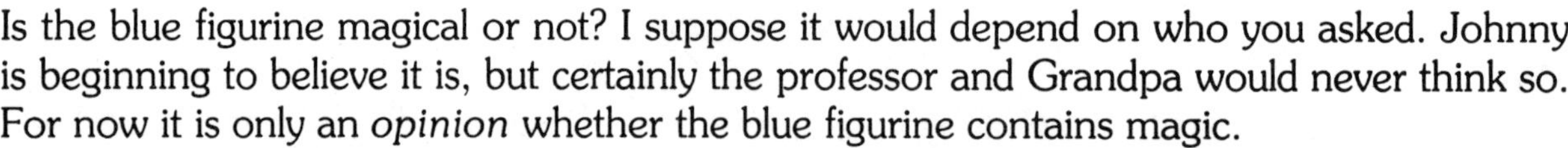

Is the blue figurine magical or not? I suppose it would depend on who you asked. Johnny is beginning to believe it is, but certainly the professor and Grandpa would never think so. For now it is only an *opinion* whether the blue figurine contains magic.

An opinion is an idea a person believes but can't prove is true. An opinion might also be someone's feelings about something or his judgement. For example, if a person thinks blue is the prettiest color, that is his opinion. In the story Johnny thought studying about ancient Egypt was very fascinating. That was his opinion because certainly not everyone believes studying ancient Egypt is fascinating. Opinions usually have judgement words in them like *good* or *bad*.

A fact is quite different from an opinion. A fact is an idea that is true or can be proved true. A fact is something that is known for certain. For example, if you say you are wearing shoes and you can look down and see them and everyone agrees that you are wearing shoes, then it is a fact that you are wearing shoes. In the story it is a fact that Johnny took the blue figurine and scroll from the church basement. We know it is a fact because he had it and he showed it to the professor. They even talked about it.

A reader of mysteries is always looking for the facts. By getting the facts he or she can usually piece together a solution to the mystery. Below are eight statements. You must decide which ones are facts and which ones are opinions. Put the letter *F* in the spaces before the ones that are facts and the letter *O* in the spaces before the ones that are opinions.

1. _____ Johnny's house was infested with spiders in March.
2. _____ Father Baart caused the death of two people.
3. _____ Eddie Tompke is a bad person.
4. _____ Robert Beard is a nice man who is only trying to help Johnny.
5. _____ The blue figurine had a label on it that said it was a souvenir of Cairo.
6. _____ Johnny had a dream in which he was being dragged into a grave by an old lady.
7. _____ Johnny's ring gives him magical powers.
8. _____ Johnny got a letter from *Hobbies* magazine telling him the mummy shaped souvenirs were sold in Cairo, Illinois, in the late 1800's.

Name_________________________ Date_______________

Chapter 8: The Curse of the Blue Figurine

Before You Read

In the last chapter Johnny let his anger and his newfound power get away from him. The result was that Eddie Tompke was blown off his feet by a mysterious wind and came down on a jagged piece of glass hurting his hand.

This was a very unusual occurrence. It was almost supernatural. Or is that just an opinion? Is it your opinion, too? It's hard to tell just what caused the tremendous wind that caused Eddie to cut himself. I wonder what Johnny would say it was? Do you think Grandpa would agree with Johnny?

On the What's Their Opinion? Work Sheet write two paragraphs. In the first one write what you think Johnny would say caused this strange wind if you interviewed him.

In the second paragraph write what you think Grandpa would say when he was told what happened that day after school. You can imagine you interviewed Grandpa, too.

As You Read

Real friends care about each other. In this first part of the chapter, Professor Childermass becomes worried about Johnny. Read to find out why he is worried and what Johnny has been doing that has his grandparents worried too.

Name______________________________ Date__________________

What's Their Opinion? Work Sheet

On the lines below, write what Johnny would say caused the strange wind that blew down Eddie Tompke and caused him to cut his hand on a broken bottle. Imagine you are Johnny being interviewed. The interview question is given below. You need to answer it as if you were Johnny.

Interviewer: We heard, Johnny, that you were by the Merrimack River when that strange wind came up and knocked over Eddie. What do you think caused such a strange happening?

____

____

____

____

____

____

____

____

____

Now imagine that you are Grandpa trying to answer the same question. Try to think like Grandpa thinks. He's a bit more skeptical than Johnny when it comes to magical things.

Interviewer: So, Grandpa, you've heard what Johnny had to say about that strange wind and how it knocked down Eddie. What do you think it was?

____

____

____

____

____

____

____

____

____

____

Name________________________________ Date________________

Chapter 8: The Curse of the Blue Figurine

After You Read

Finding Details

Living inside a nightmare...that's what it's been like for Johnny.

That explanation of Johnny's life is found in Chapter 8. The rest of that page and the next page go on to describe why Johnny feels like he has been living in a nightmare. On your own paper pick out the details that help explain why Johnny feels this way.

The first one can be found in the very next paragraph. It says that *Johnny felt he had to say the prayer to Thoth and Toueris every day, but he didn't know why*. In other words, Johnny felt compelled to do something he wasn't even sure he wanted to do.

See if you can find at least five more details. If you're good, you will be able to find eight more.

1. ______________________________
2. ______________________________
3. ______________________________
4. ______________________________
5. ______________________________
6. ______________________________
7. ______________________________
8. ______________________________

Name____ Date____________________

The Curse of the Blue Figurine

Sequencing

Read over the following sentences. Each sentence is a part from Chapter 8. Altogether these sentences make up the episode you read in Chapter 8. It is your job to unscramble the sentences so that they form a paragraph that summarizes Chapter 8.

Begin by unscrambling the sentences and putting them in the correct order. Write a 1 in front of the sentence that tells what happened first in the chapter, a 2 in front of the sentence that tells what happened second and so on. Finally, on your own paper write them as a complete paragraph in paragraph form. Remember to indent.

Just for fun, in each sentence there is a capitalization error. When you rewrite the sentences as a paragraph, try to correct the words that have not been capitalized and should be.

_____ Mr. Beard admitted that the ring was magical and raised his hand which caused johnny's arm to hurt terribly.

_____ the professor was worried because he had not seen or heard from Johnny in a couple of weeks.

_____ As mr. Beard laughed, his features and clothing began to change.

_____ He decided to wait ten minutes there for mr. Beard and then leave.

_____ Professor Childermass was working on putting up an aerial that he read about in *mechanix illustrated*.

_____ the three of them cooked up a plan that allowed the professor to follow Johnny the next time he went out.

_____ So, professor Childermass went over to Grandma and Grandpa's house to talk to them about Johnny.

_____ When Johnny got to the church, he found a note that told him to go to duston park so he went there.

_____ That evening Johnny told Grandma and Grandpa that he would be going to st. michael's church.

_____ Eventually mr. Beard showed up in what seemed a bad mood.

_____ as Johnny left his house, the professor began to tail him.

Name______________________________ Date__________________

Chapter 9: The Curse of the Blue Figurine

Before You Read

Mr. Beard's face changed to the face of an old man with an overhanging forehead, a hawkish nose and deep-set eyes. He was wearing the collar of a Catholic priest around his neck.

That description sounds pretty familiar. Have you guessed who it is yet? Well the mystery isn't over with.

The description above can bring to mind a very sinister-looking person–someone who appears evil. Since the book does not have illustrations, we have to imagine for ourselves what each character looks like.

Below is the outline of a face. Using the description above, fill in the facial features to create an image of the face Johnny was looking at.

As You Read

All right, so you are now convinced that Johnny is indeed caught up in a ghostly mystery. Or is he? In Chapter 9 Johnny visits a psychiatrist who hypnotizes him and tries to convince him that he really is imagining all these things. Read to find out what happens when Johnny gets hypnotized and think about whether you believe Johnny's experience is real or imaginary.

Name______________________________________ Date__________________

The Curse of the Blue Figurine

Similes

Good mysteries are able to create vivid pictures in our minds. We can imagine the creepy feeling Johnny had exploring in St. Michael's Church basement. We can imagine what Duston Park looked like that mysterious evening when Johnny met with Mr. Beard. One of the reasons we can imagine these things is because of the way John Bellairs uses language in his story. He uses many descriptions. One of the descriptions he uses is a figure of speech called a simile.

A simile is a comparison between two things using the words *like* or *as*. For example, if you wrote that Eddie was as strong *as* a bull, you would be comparing Eddie to a bull. Another example can be seen in this sentence: The professor was quiet *like* a church mouse. In that example the professor was compared to a church mouse. In both sentences the words *like* or *as* were used in the comparison.

The Curse of the Blue Figurine has many similes. Below are the beginnings of some of them found in Chapters 8 and 9. You are to find them and fill in the missing parts of the comparison. Include the page number where you found the simile.

Example: When Johnny met with Mr. Beard in Duston Park, "He felt *like* some small frightened animal caught in a trap." p. 118

Chapter 8

1. Eddie Tompke began to avoid Johnny *like*

   ____ p. ____

2. Johnny was afraid that the blue figurine would come waddling out *like*

   ____ p. ____

3. When Mr. Beard raised his hand, Johnny's whole left arm felt *as*

   ____ p. ____

Chapter 9

4. When talking with his grandparents, Johnny felt that the ring was *like*

   ____ p. ____

5. In Johnny's mind his Friday appointment with Mr. Beard was *like*

   ____ p. ____

6. The professor said that Johnny's grandparents were as poor *as*

   ____ p. ____

Name______________________________ Date______________

The Curse of the Blue Figurine

Decision Making

Well, it's time to make a decision. Most of the facts are in. You just need to sort through them, evaluate them and come to a conclusion.

The question is:
Is Johnny really caught up in a ghostly adventure?

or

Is Johnny just imagining that these things are happening to him?

It isn't an easy decision to make. There are good arguments for each side.

To help you decide, fill out the Decision Making Work Sheet. It will help you sort out the clues and guide you to a conclusion.

Then on your own paper write a paragraph in which you argue why you either believe Johnny is part of a ghostly mystery or believe this is all his imagination.

Be prepared to defend and argue your point when you are done. This assignement is due

______________________.

Name________________________________ Date________________

Decision Making Work Sheet

The first step is to list all the reasons on each side of the argument. When you do this you must try to make as complete a list on each side as you can. List every reason even if you don't believe it or if you can think of an argument against it. The idea is to list all reasons not just the ones you believe in. Below are spaces for this. Use your own paper if you run out of room.

Reasons to Believe That Johnny Is Involved in a Ghostly Mystery	Reasons to Believe That This Is Only Johnny's Imagination
______________________________	______________________________
______________________________	______________________________
______________________________	______________________________
______________________________	______________________________
______________________________	______________________________
______________________________	______________________________
______________________________	______________________________
______________________________	______________________________
______________________________	______________________________
______________________________	______________________________
______________________________	______________________________
______________________________	______________________________
______________________________	______________________________
______________________________	______________________________
______________________________	______________________________
______________________________	______________________________

Now look over both lists and decide which reasons you find most convincing. That will help you decide which side you believe.

When you have decided which side you believe in, prepare a paragraph on your own paper in which you argue why you believe in that side. Not only should you give reasons to believe in that side, but you should also give reasons not to believe the other side.

Be prepared to argue your decision.

Name________________________________ Date__________________

Chapter 10: The Curse of the Blue Figurine

Planning

Before You Read

Johnny is going on a trip. The professor is going to take him to the White Mountains of New Hampshire.

Hopefully such a trip will get Johnny's mind off of the statue and the ghost.

Going on a trip requires quite a bit of planning.

You have to plan the route, where you're going to stay and get everything packed that you need to take.

Imagine you were going to take a relaxing vacation to somewhere in the United States. Assume you were going to travel by car.

Plan a trip to that spot. Your plans do not have to be too detailed, but they must include the following things:

1. A list of all the things that you will be packing to take with you, including all clothing and how much of it you will take.

2. Your destination and what route you plan on following to get there. You'll need a map for that.

Use your own paper to come up with your list and your route.

This assignment is due ______________________________.

Name________________________________ Date________________

Chapter 10: The Curse of the Blue Figurine

As You Read

Most good mysteries build up the suspense and then let it down. Then they build it up a little more and let it down again. That is what we've been experiencing so far in this story. With Johnny's visit to Dr. Melkonian, the suspense was let down because we once again had reason to believe that Johnny was just imagining everything.

Well, have you noticed, the story isn't over yet? So we can prepare ourselves for another build-up of suspense. In this chapter read to see what happens as Johnny and the professor begin to relax on their vacation.

After You Read

Memory Buster

Once you have finished reading Chapter 10, close your book and try to answer the questions below. When you have answered all you can, open your book and verify your answers and fill in any you missed. Put the page number where you found the answer on the line after the question.

1. The professor and Johnny are headed for the Hag View Cottages by Hellbent Mountain. In what state is this place? p. _____

   ____

2. Why is Johnny so entranced by the sight of mountains? p. _____

   ____

3. What is "The Hag"? p. _____

   ____

4. What does the professor need that causes him to leave Johnny? p. _____

   ____

5. What did Johnny see that scared him out of his wits? p. _____

   ____

6. Who enters the room after Johnny and the professor are asleep? p. _____

   ____

7. What does this uninvited guest get Johnny to do? p. _____

   ____

Name______________________________ Date______________

Chapter 10: The Curse of the Blue Figurine

Before You Read

If you had decided that all of this was just Johnny's imagination, you were wrong. It looks as if there really is a ghost, and it is definitely after Johnny. The question is why? On the lines below explain why you think the ghost is after Johnny and what he wants.

____

____

____

____

____

As You Read

All along in this story we have been getting clues. There was a note left by Father Baart before he disappeared. That was very important. You may want to go back and reread it, and then go on to Chapter 11 in order to find out what happens to Johnny and how the professor figures it all out. Also pay attention to how the professor's dream helps Johnny.

Name______________________________ Date__________________

Chapter 11: The Curse of the Blue Figurine

After You Read

Cause and Effect

With cause and effect order, one event causes another to occur. Read the beginning of each sentence below. Finish it by writing what should come after the word *because*.

Example: Johnny arose and walked out of the room in the middle of the night *because* the ghost of Father Baart put the ring back on him and controlled him.

1. The professor realized Johnny could not have made up his story *because*
____
2. At first the professor is able to follow Johnny *because*
____
3. When the paths split, the professor knew which one to follow *because*
____
4. The professor is able to ward off the ghost *because*
____
5. Johnny comes to his senses *because*
____
6. After thinking about the note Father Baart left before he disappeared, the professor begins digging in the cave *because* he realizes
____
7. The professor is unable to hold off the ghost *because*
____

Name________________________________ Date________________

Chapter 12: The Curse of the Blue Figurine

As You Read

If you're keeping score, it's the ghost of Father Baart–1, the good guys–0.

This can't be the end! Read to find out what happened to Professor Childermass and what's going to happen to Johnny and Father Baart.

After You Read

After reading Chapter 1 you listed all the characters that had appeared in the story up to that point. If you go back over that list, you'll notice that many of them are still in the story helping to move the action along. Some of the characters have become more important than others. These are called main characters.

On the lines below, decide who you think are the main characters in this story. There is room for you to select five main characters, but that doesn't mean there really are that many. You should have at least two, but you may want more. After each one write your reasons why you think that person should be considered a main character of this story.

1. ______________ ____

____

2. ______________ ____

____

3. ______________ ____

____

4. ______________ ____

____

5. ______________ ____

____

On the lines below list any other characters that you think are important but not necessarily main characters.

______________ ______________ ______________

______________ ______________ ______________

Name________________________________ Date________________

The Curse of the Blue Figurine

Reading Maps

Many of the places mentioned in this story really exist. Below is a list of these places. Using an atlas found in your classroom or library, locate these places and put them on The Curse of the Blue Figurine Map.

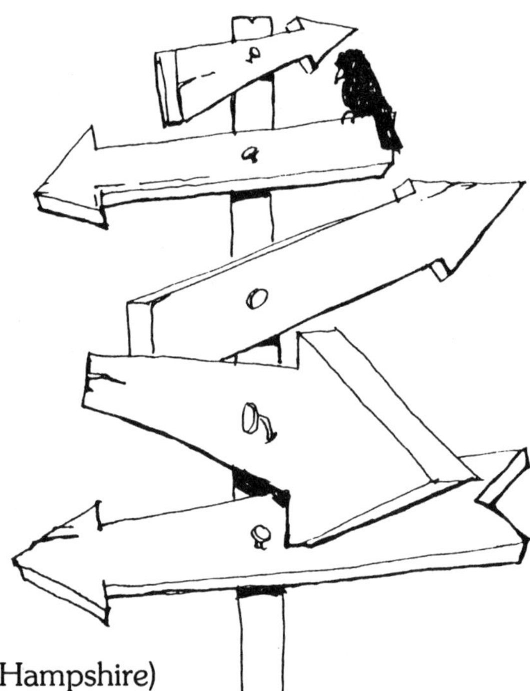

1. Merrimack River, Massachusetts
2. Riverhead, Long Island, New York
3. Franconia, New Hampshire
4. Franconian Notch
5. Gale River, New Hampshire
6. The Presidential Range
   Mt. Washington
   Mt. Jefferson
7. U.S. Route 3
8. White Mountains, New Hampshire
9. Cambridge, Massachusetts
10. Rochester, New Hampshire
11. Durham, New Hampshire (University of New Hampshire)

Several places are not real. Duston Heights, Massachusetts, and Hellbent Mountain, New Hampshire, appear to be made up. Based on what you've read, place these two locations on your map.

Name____ Date____________________

The Curse of the Blue Figurine Map

Supplemental Vocabulary

Not all the lessons contain vocabulary work. Nonetheless, you may want to supplement your teaching with additional vocabulary work from time to time. Below are additional lists of vocabulary words by chapters. Those chapters that have vocabulary development in the lessons already are omitted. No more than seven words per chapter are included, but you may find more by looking through the chapter yourself.

Chapter 1

1. bespectacled
2. parlor
3. register
4. fedora
5. rector
6. talisman
7. obscure

Chapter 3

1. lunged
2. incinerator
3. awestruck
4. bided
5. peevishly
6. rant
7. rampart

Chapter 4

1. humiliated
2. bona fide
3. forlornly
4. sheepish
5. disparaging
6. contented

Chapter 6

1. genuflected
2. gilded
3. musty
4. prosperous
5. uncanny
6. monogram
7. sentimental

Chapter 8

1. aerial
2. scaffold
3. diabetes
4. insulin
5. shadow
6. amulet
7. shrouded

Chapter 9

1. torment
2. wanly
3. somber
4. jaunty
5. indignantly
6. sodium pentothal
7. dislocations

Chapter 10

1. entranced
2. foreboding
3. grievement
4. sinister
5. placidly
6. glowered
7. specters

Chapter 11

1. plodded
2. beetling
3. insane
4. tinder
5. cairn
6. interred
7. disintegrated

Chapter 12

1. din
2. dislodged
3. chasm
4. ushered
5. charred
6. pedantic
7. torte

Words Related to Archaeology and Ancient Egypt

1. archaeology
2. Egyptologist
3. pharaoh
4. hieroglyphs
5. ushabti
6. mummy
7. Thoth
8. Toueris
9. crook
10. flail
11. Kush

Extension Activities

Radio Programs

Johnny Dixon liked to listen to radio programs like "The House of Mystery." Students today know nothing of the radio programs of the 1940's and early 1950's. As a starter get one of the records that features episodes from some of these radio programs from the local library. Allow students to listen to them and discuss what the characters must look like and what the action must look like. They can also illustrate a scene from one of these programs. Have them discuss how some of the sound effects might have been created. Unlike today, most of those live radio broadcasts have many articles available to create the sounds of doors closing, shoes walking on wooden floors, etc.

Variation

Once students have had a chance to listen to some of these programs, they can begin looking for ways to create sound effects of their own. Many common items can be used to make the sounds because the audience only hears but doesn't see. It will get students tuned into sounds and not sights. Have them then create a collection of sounds from dripping water in a sink to someone sweeping the floor to shuffling feet, and so on.

Variation

If students really get into it, they can produce their own radio program. Have them script out some simple bedtime story like "Little Red Riding Hood" or "Goldilocks and the Three Bears." It won't be hard if they get one of the many picture books with the story already scripted out. They can rehearse the parts, plan the sound effects and finally perform the show on tape for playback in class. If you can get something to act as a screen, they may be able to perform live behind the screen with the audience just listening.

If you are interested in this last project, realize that it must be approached gradually. I have found the students to experience less frustration and enjoy more success during the production when they have first heard old-time radio programs, then experimented with sound effects and voices and finally put the production together.

Souvenirs

Johnny thought that he had a worthless souvenir. Souvenirs can be found in anyone's house who has ever traveled outside the limits of his own town. In many cases souvenirs are even handed down and ultimately stored in the attic, basement, etc. Have the students design a souvenir display for the classroom. In it would be some of the souvenirs they have accumulated on their own or parents' trips. Each item can have a small card in front of it telling where it is from, when it was obtained and whose it is.

You can then have each select one of his souvenirs and write down the trip that led to the purchase of the souvenir. These too can be shared in class.

Chapter Titles and Illustrations: See page 162.

Dreams

John Bellairs relies on dreams to help develop the plot of this story. Johnny has dreams about Father Baart and a curio shop, and the professor has a dream that ultimately gets him to realize that Johnny's story about a ghost is true. Students love to tell about their dreams. They've all had them, especially the recurring kind where they're flying, falling or meeting someone.

Have a dream-telling session. Since the session will rely on telling and not reading, the students must work out the details of their dreams in advance. The point is to get them to tell their dreams in as much detail as possible, not just giving the basic gist. A small lesson on what kind of detail to include should be conducted first. Have students reread the dreams that Johnny has. Notice the descriptions of the characters, the explanation of the feelings Johnny has, the detail of events and sights. That's the kind of storytelling the students will be aiming for.

Design a Blue Figurine

The ancient Egyptian culture really did believe that objects buried with the deceased could be carried to the afterlife. Other ancient civilizations believed the same thing. Unfortunately, some civilizations carried the idea a bit too far and often killed servants to be buried with the royalty in order that they act as servants in the afterlife.

With a little clay or plasticene, students can create their own blue figurines. In fact they may want to design two. One could be a representation of the blue figurine mentioned in the story. Another could be a representation of the type of person he would want buried with him to travel to the afterlife.

Money Raiser

The students at Johnny's school held a paper drive to earn money. Using the Productive Thinking Guidelines sheet found on page 140, have students brainstorm for other ways a class could earn money for a school project. Make a chart of possible answers and display it.

As part of a planning activity, students could even work out the details of carrying out one of the fund-raisers. Have them list the steps so that they can understand that these kind of projects do not just happen, but often must be developed step-by-step.

Most fund-raising ideas fall into two categories–rendering services (like the good old-fashion car wash) or selling products (like candy sales, used book sales, etc.). Have students think these ideas through as to their relative advantages or disadvantages (service fund-raisers have low overhead but require time; product sales require an overhead but not as much physical labor). Have them investigate needed supplies, materials, time, number of people, sources of materials, etc. All this can be charted, and in the end they can project a possible profit margin.

This is a great activity to go along with any career education requirements your curriculum may have.

Reports on Egypt: See page 80.

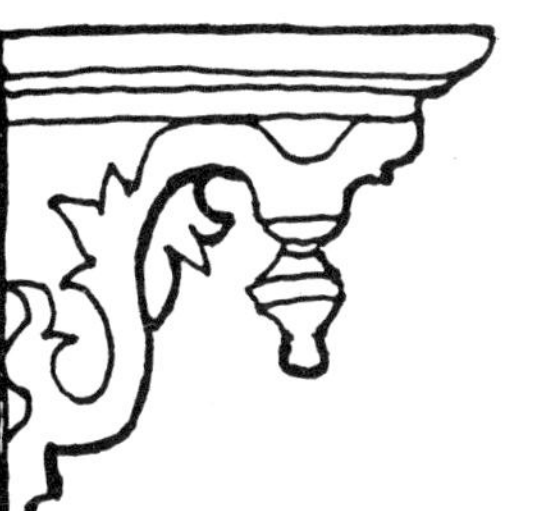

The House of Dies Drear

by

Virginia Hamilton

As the story begins, Thomas Small is traveling to Ohio from North Carolina where his father has accepted a new position at a college as a professor. During the ride, Thomas rehashes much of the information about the house into which they will move. We learn that the house was once owned by a man named Dies Drear, who was a conductor on the underground railroad. Dies Drear was a mysterious, eccentric man who collected priceless antiques but kept his abolitionist role a secret. He was found out and murdered. A legend then began to grow that the house was haunted by his spirit along with the spirits of two slaves whom he had been hiding at the time. Eventually the house's ownership passed into the hands of a foundation who employed a caretaker known only as Mr. Pluto.

When they arrive Thomas' feelings of uneasiness about the house are only enhanced. First he meets two children who live in the community and address him strangely. Then he gets lost in a secret passageway beneath the house and must be rescued by his father. Finally, he meets the enigmatic Mr. Pluto who mistakes him for a trespasser when he stumbles upon Mr. Pluto's living quarters, a cave located on the grounds. Mr. Pluto apologizes for scaring Thomas, but his mysterious air leaves the family feeling unsure of his intentions.

The next day the Small family continues to encounter bizarre events including warnings to get out, suspicious greetings in church and an encounter with a much friendlier but more feeble Mr. Pluto. When the Smalls arrive home and find their house vandalized, Mr. Small becomes convinced the mysterious Mr. Pluto is at fault. He and Thomas go to confront Mr. Pluto at the cave, but he disappears.

While looking around they discover a false wall and its trip lever and enter a whole new section of the cave that extends below the grounds. This section of the cave is filled with museum-quality artifacts collected by the real Dies Drear during his life. They also encounter the more feeble version of Mr. Pluto who tells them that many years ago he discovered this wealth of antiques and has been keeping it a secret. At the same time another Mr. Pluto arrives who turns out to be his son, Mayhew. Mayhew had returned to help his father upon learning that his father's health had taken a turn for the worse and would be unable to fend off constant attempts of the Darrow family to find the "treasure." Grandfather Darrow, it seems, mistakenly believes he has a claim to it. Disguised as his father, Mayhew continued to scare off the trespassing Darrows the same as his father had done for years.

Mr. Small and Thomas then become involved in a plot and a bit of tomfoolery designed to scare and embarrass the Darrow family. It was the Darrows who vandalized the Small home and had also perpetrated the warnings they received in an effort to scare them out. The plan works and in the end Mr. Small decides not to report the treasure of artifacts until they can all be cataloged and studied, a job that will keep everything a secret for a long, long time to come.

Name________________________________ Date________________

Chapter 1: The House of Dies Drear

Before You Read

If you've ever had to move you know that it can be both exciting and scary. It's exciting because you'll be going somewhere new and having new experiences. On the other hand it is scary because you're leaving behind friends and familiar places. Of course, where you are moving to has a lot to do with how you are going to feel.

Imagine you had the *choice* to move wherever you wanted. Where would you choose to go? Your only limit is that you must stay within the country. Fill in the lines below as they relate to your fantasy move. Be prepared to share your answers and explain them.

1. Given a choice, I would move to________________________________
2. My reason for moving to that place is because________________________
____
3. In moving to this place the thing I would most look forward to is ____________
____
4. The thing I would most regret leaving behind would be ________________
____
5. The one thing I own that I would want to take with me is ______________
____

Just for fun let's imagine the opposite. Where is the last place in this country to which you would want to move?________________________________

What is your reason?________________________________

____

As You Read

You may have read some stories that have taken a while to get started. That's not true of *The House of Dies Drear*. The mystery begins almost immediately. Thomas Small is traveling with his family to a new home in Ohio. The story begins with a very strange dream he is having.

Read Chapter 1 to find out what kind of dream Thomas has and try to figure out how it might relate to where they are moving. Also pay attention to information you get about the kind of place *from where* they are moving and the kind of place *to where* they are moving.

Name____ Date____________________

Chapter 1: The House of Dies Drear

After You Read

All stories including mysteries have certain elements that are the same. These include the setting, the characters and the plot. We are introduced to all three in this first chapter. Complete each section in order to learn more about these three elements in *The House of Dies Drear*. All questions should be answered on your own paper. Each set of answers should have the same title as the heading.

Setting

The setting of a story is the time and place of the story. Although the setting can change from chapter to chapter and even within a chapter, the general setting rarely changes throughout the book.

1. Where are the characters of the story as it opens?
2. From where is the Small family traveling?
3. To where are they headed?
4. Find two clues in Chapter 1 that the story takes place in the present.

Characters

The characters of the story are the people involved in the story. Most of the time they are regular, human being-type people, but in some stories they may be animals, spirits, houses, etc. In the first chapter of a story we are usually introduced to some of the most important characters and given a little background about each. Answer these questions about the characters introduced in Chapter 1.

1. What is Mrs. Small's attitude toward the move they are making?
2. What is Mr. Small's profession and education?
3. How old is Thomas, and what is one of his hobbies?
4. How can you tell that Thomas is to be one of the main characters of the story?
5. What proof is there that the twins are very young?

Plot

The plot is what happens in the story. It is the action of the story. Although little real action has happened so far, you have gotten background information that will help you unravel the mystery of the story.

1. Briefly recount the dream Thomas has.
2. Dreams sometimes act as warnings. What warning might Thomas be receiving in this dream?
3. What interesting historical facts have we learned about the house the Small family will be moving into?

Name______________________ Date______________

Chapter 2: The House of Dies Drear

As You Read

The dream and the little we know about the house the Smalls are moving into help provide some mystery in Chapter 1. In Chapter 2 the mystery widens to include not only the house but the legend behind it. Read Chapter 2 to learn more about the house of Dies Drear as well as the man himself. Pay particular attention to characters who are mentioned as part of the legend and part of the house's history.

After You Read

The underground railroad is a real part of our country's history. The underground railroad existed prior to 1861 before slavery was abolished. The actual term *underground railroad* has nothing to do with railroads. The term came about because it was a secret (underground) network of people who helped runaway slaves make their way north (railroad) to free states and Canada. By reading this story you will get a lot of information about it.

Context Clues

It is sometimes possible to figure out what a word means because of the way it is used in a sentence or paragraph. Any clue found in a story that allows you to understand the meaning of a word is called a context clue.

Below are some important words related to the underground railroad and the story. In the space after each word or term, write a definition in your own wording based on context clues.

1. stations: ______________________

____

2. bondage: ______________________

____

3. maneuvering money: ______________________

____

4. selah: ______________________

____

5. bounty hunters: ______________________

____

6. freeman's community: ______________________

____

Name_______________________________________ Date____________________

Chapters 1 and 2: The House of Dies Drear

A Mystery Unfolds

Facts, opinions, legends, stories, reports. You've been exposed to all of these so far in the story. All of them are helping to shape what is becoming the mystery. Being a good reader of mysteries means being able to identify parts of the story that help to create the mystery. These are the unexplained or unexplainable parts of the story.

On the other hand, it is equally important to correctly identify the facts of the story because they will help you focus on a solution to the mystery.

Below is a set of sentences about the story. All of them are facts but some are statements that help to create the mystery. Sort them out as mysteries or facts by placing an *F* in front of the ones that are purely facts and an *M* in front of the ones that help create mystery.

_____ The house the Smalls are moving into was built by a man who helped runaway slaves.

_____ Thomas has a dream in which he is chased by a man with white hair and red eyes and is told to stay away.

_____ The foundation report mentioned a legend that said the house of Dies Drear was haunted by ghosts.

_____ The house has a caretaker named Mr. Pluto.

_____ Mr. Pluto's name is a reference to the Lord of the Underworld.

_____ Mr. Pluto's description matches that of the man in Thomas' dream.

_____ Thomas is told by his father to never mention the third slave.

_____ The plans to the house have been missing for years.

_____ Mr. Small hopes to buy the house some day.

_____ No one has lived in the house for more than three months over the past one hundred years.

_____ Thomas believes his father meant to hide the legend from him.

_____ Mr. Pluto rides around in a two-wheeled horse and buggy.

A Mystery Reader's Notebook

Begin keeping a notebook of strange or curious facts that you notice as you read this story. Every so often check what you've written down in order to help piece the mystery together.

Name______________________________ Date________________

Chapter 3: The House of Dies Drear

Before You Read

Thomas is convinced that the house of Dies Drear is haunted. Haunted houses. What do they look like? What do they sound, smell, feel like? Most people can get a clear image in their head when asked to imagine a haunted house. Not everyone imagines exactly the same thing, but certain images are very similar. On the outside perhaps you imagine *peeling paint* or *creaking steps*. Inside you might imagine a *musty-smelling room*. These italicized words are all phrases that help describe the sights, sounds, smells and feel of a haunted house.

Notice that each of the italicized descriptive phrases is made up of two parts: something being described (paint, steps, room) and words to describe it (peeling, creaking, musty-smelling). On the lines below create your own descriptive phrases for a haunted house. In doing so try to focus on all the senses and not just the sense of sight. Be prepared to share your ideas in class.

Descriptions of the Land the Haunted House Is On

_______________ _______________ _______________

_______________ _______________ _______________

_______________ _______________ _______________

Descriptions of the Outside of the Haunted House

_______________ _______________ _______________

_______________ _______________ _______________

_______________ _______________ _______________

Descriptions of the Inside of the Haunted House

_______________ _______________ _______________

_______________ _______________ _______________

_______________ _______________ _______________

Using these wonderfully descriptive phrases, put together a paragraph that describes your haunted house. You are not limited to just these phrases. You may add more descriptions as you go along.

A drawing should accompany the paragraph. Your drawing can be of the outside of the house or one of the rooms inside. Make your drawing in pencil using only shading to create the spooky feeling.

Name______________________________________ Date__________________

Chapter 3: The House of Dies Drear

As You Read

After so much talk about the house of Dies Drear, Thomas finally gets the opportunity to see it and enter it. As you read this chapter try to visualize the house of Dies Drear as Thomas sees it. Notice that the descriptions begin with the land surrounding the house; then focus on the outside of the house and finally on the inside of it.

The mystery continues to mount in this chapter as well. Pay attention to the unexplainable reaction the twins have to the house and finally to the hidden button Thomas finds.

After You Read

Architecture

Many words are used in describing the house of Dies Drear that you may not be familiar with. These include mansard roof, veranda, dormer and dormer window, pillars, foyer, eaves and quatrefoil.

On your own paper, create a visual dictionary of these words. Write the word, and then draw a picture or diagram of each one.

Description

Just as you developed your image of a haunted house with descriptive phrases, so too did Virginia Hamilton. Look over the first half of the chapter again and in the spaces below list interesting descriptive phrases she used to create Thomas' haunting image of the house of Dies Drear.

The Land Surrounding the House

____________________ ____________________ ____________________

____________________ ____________________ ____________________

____________________ ____________________ ____________________

The House Itself

____________________ ____________________ ____________________

____________________ ____________________ ____________________

____________________ ____________________ ____________________

Name_______________________________ Date_________________

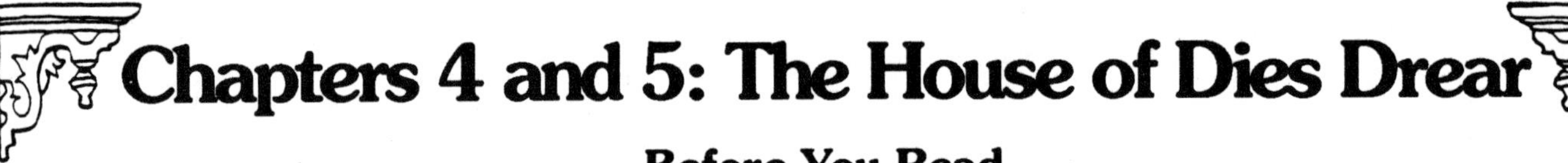

Chapters 4 and 5: The House of Dies Drear

Before You Read

When Thomas turned around he saw the strangest thing he had ever seen in his life. What was it? Certainly there are many possibilities considering the legends he's read about. On the lines below, write the description of what you imagine Thomas saw.

As You Read

Altogether, Chapters 4 and 5 are three episodes. The first episode is made up of what Thomas saw and the most peculiar meeting that it led to. The second episode is made up of his terrifying tunnel adventure. The last episode involves Thomas' family and his attempt to get them to understand what he heard and saw.

As you read these two chapters, group the events into these three episodes in order to more easily follow the action of the story.

Name____ Date____________________

Chapters 4 and 5: The House of Dies Drear

After You Read

Sequencing

Below are ten sentences from the two chapters you just read. Put them in the order in which they happened by writing a 1 in front of the sentence that tells what happened first, a 2 in front of the sentence that tells what happened second and so on. Do this with the book closed and put your answers in the first set of spaces. Then check your answers and make any sequence changes in the second set of spaces.

_____ _____ Frantically, Thomas screams for help and has another tunnel wall slide open into the kitchen.

_____ _____ Thomas discovers long stone slabs that he thinks could have been used by runaway slaves.

_____ _____ Thomas sees a small girl riding a big black horse followed by a big boy holding the horse's tail.

_____ _____ Thomas gets permission to explore the outside of the house in order to get a better understanding of where tunnels might be.

_____ _____ Thomas loses his flashlight and begins to hear an AHHHHHH sound.

_____ _____ Thomas falls into the tunnel.

_____ _____ Mr. and Mrs. Small listen doubtfully to Thomas' story.

_____ _____ Thomas thinks to use his pencil-thin flashlight that he always carries with him.

_____ _____ Mr. Small explores the tunnel and then disconnects the mechanism that allows the walls to open up into the tunnel.

_____ _____ Thomas learns that the small girl's name is Pesty and the boy is Mac Darrow and that they both know Mr. Pluto.

Name_______________________________________ Date___________________

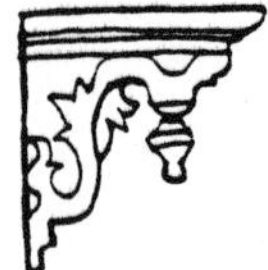

The House of Dies Drear

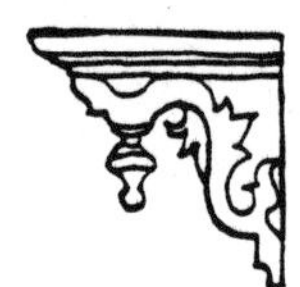

Point of View

Throughout the story so far Thomas has been the main character. All the events and episodes have happened through him. As a result we know not only what he has said and done but also what he has been thinking. Unfortunately Thomas does not always say what he is thinking. In fact, he sometimes hides his thoughts and says the opposite.

At the end of Chapter 5 Thomas suspects that his father is hiding something from him. He even suspects that Mr. Small dislikes Mr. Pluto's arrangement of the house. Nonetheless, he does not say these thoughts. On the lines below write what Thomas says in your own words.

____

____

Several times throughout the story Thomas has kept his thoughts hidden. Skim Chapters 2, 3 and 5 in order to find at least two other instances. On the lines below record what these secret thoughts and opinions are in complete sentences. Pay particular attention to Thomas' feelings about Mr. Pluto, the legend and the house. Before each one list the page and paragraph number where you found it.

1. page _____ paragraph _____ ____

____

____

____

2. page _____ paragraph _____ ____

____

____

____

It wouldn't be hard to imagine that Mr. or Mrs. Small had secret thoughts or opinions of their own. On your own paper write a few sentences that might be the thoughts of Mr. or Mrs. Small and their feelings about the house, the legend or Mr. Pluto.

Name______________________________________ Date____________________

The House of Dies Drear

Decision Making

Throughout the development of this mystery, one name keeps coming up. That name is Mr. Pluto. In Chapter 1 he was present as a dream character. Since then he has been constantly in Thomas' thoughts and in the goings-on of each episode.

So what is your impression of this man? Is he the devil that his name implies or a helpful caretaker? You must make the decision, but first you must weigh what you know against what you only think you know.

The first step in decision making is to make a list of all the available information. You can do that on the lines below. Begin with Chapter 1 and in a word or phrase, list everything you've learned about Mr. Pluto whether you know it to be true or not.

______________________________ ______________________________

______________________________ ______________________________

______________________________ ______________________________

______________________________ ______________________________

______________________________ ______________________________

______________________________ ______________________________

The second step in decision making is to sort out the information. You can begin by separating the factual information from the information that is more imaginative. Look over your list and put a star by any item about Mr. Pluto that you know is true.

Sometimes we make decisions based on a "gut feeling" or intuition. Look over the list one more time and put a check mark by any item that you can't prove is true, but your instincts tell you is true.

The last step is to combine all these ideas into a final decision. When you have decided what kind of a person Mr. Pluto is, write a paragraph in which you explain your decision. Include your opinion of the man in the first sentence, and then write several more sentences supporting your idea. Refer to the story in explaining your ideas. Be ready to share this in class.

Name____ Date____________________

Chapters 6 and 7: The House of Dies Drear

As You Read

It's time to meet the famous or infamous Mr. Pluto. You may have come to realize that you know very little about this man for sure. Almost everything you know is either rumor or imagined. Only by becoming acquainted with him personally will you (or Thomas) be able to make a sound decision. One thing is for sure. The mystery surrounding the house of Dies Drear is linked to Mr. Pluto.

After You Read

Have you ever come across a word that has more than one meaning? How do you know which one to use? Chances are you just see how the word is used in the sentence and make your decision that way. Below are ten words found in Chapters 6 and 7. They are listed in the order in which they appear. After each is a possible definition. Decide which definition is the correct one by checking the book and seeing how the word was used. Circle the correct definition.

Chapter 6

1. shoot: to move swiftly; to dart **or** the young buds of a plant
2. dozed: to move large amounts of earth **or** to nap lightly
3. jowls: the cheeks **or** inside the jaw
4. notion: any small household item **or** a general impression or feeling
5. threshold: a piece of wood placed beneath a door **or** the beginning point

Chapter 7

6. cordial: pleasant and sincere **or** a sweet alcoholic drink
7. shifty: able to move easily from position to position **or** crafty in appearance
8. stock: animals kept on a farm **or** completely or totally
9. bay: an opening or recess in the wall **or** a reddish-brown horse
10. hobble: to tie an animal's feet in order to restrain it **or** to walk with a limp as if one is lame

Name________________________________ Date____________________

The House of Dies Drear

Finding Details

The first thing out of Thomas' mouth when Mr. Pluto sticks his head out of the ground is the word *devil*! All in all, it isn't surprising that Thomas would react this way. So many little details created the image of Mr. Pluto being a devil that in the excitement of the moment Thomas would certainly have believed it to be so.

On the lines below see if you can recall what those details are. List details from the story that create the image of Mr. Pluto being a devil. You will find many in Chapter 6, but you will not want to stop there. Look back at previous chapters to get at some of the more interesting ones. List at least six. Include page numbers where you found the details.

1. ______________________________
2. ______________________________
3. ______________________________
4. ______________________________
5. ______________________________
6. ______________________________
7. ______________________________
8. ______________________________
9. ______________________________
10. ______________________________

Name________________________________ Date____________________

Chapters 6 and 7: The House of Dies Drear

As You Read

It's getting late and time for bed in the Small household. It's been an exciting day, but nighttime in the house of Dies Drear could prove to be even more mysterious.

This chapter has two distinct episodes. In the first episode, Thomas, his mom and dad sit around and discuss the encounter with Mr. Pluto. As you read notice Mr. Small's comments, spoken to himself, about Mr. Pluto. The second part of the chapter deals with Thomas' room. Read to find out what Thomas thinks of his room, where he sleeps and what happens in the house after he falls asleep.

Thomas' Room

As Thomas entered his room he was almost blinded by the light given off by the globe light. The rest of his room is explained in careful detail including what everything looked like and where it was.

In the space below, diagram Thomas' room as you imagine it from the reading. You need not draw the furniture as it is described. You can use geometric shapes (squares, rectangles, etc.) to represent the items. Be sure to place objects as they are described in the chapter and label all items in your diagram. The door to the room is at the bottom of the page.

Name________________________________ Date____________________

Chapter 8: The House of Dies Drear

After You Read

Memory Buster

After you've read this chapter and feel you understand it, close the book and see what you can recall about it from memory. Don't look in the book until you have answered as many questions as possible. When you are done, open your book and check the answers you've written. Put the page number where you find that answer in the space after the question. Fill in any missing answers.

1. Several things about his encounter with Mr. Pluto bothered Mr. Small. What was one of these things? p. _____

   ____

2. What was Thomas allowed to have because it was his birthday? p. _____

   ____

3. Why will Mr. Small have little luck getting a lock tomorrow? p. _____

   ____

4. What does Thomas dislike about the location of his room? p. _____

   ____

5. What is in Thomas' room that bothers him so much? p. _____

   ____

6. Where does Thomas go to sleep? p. _____

   ____

7. How did the mysterious figure enter the house? p. _____

   ____

8. What does the mysterious figure do after entering the house? p. _____

   ____

Name______________________________ Date______________

Chapter 9: The House of Dies Drear

As You Read

A mysterious person entered the house while Thomas and the Smalls slept and left something outside each door upstairs. So it would seem the mystery continues. In this chapter some questions are answered that have been part of the mystery for a while. Unfortunately, some new questions come up. That's the way it is with a mystery. Two steps forward and one step back.

First read to find out what was left by the mysterious stranger and how Mr. Small reacts to it. That's the new mysterious part of the chapter. Then read about the second encounter Thomas and Mr. Small have with Mr. Pluto. That's when Thomas gets some of the mystery solved.

After You Read

Explain It

To help you sort out this information, answer each question below on your own paper. Answer in full sentences and be ready to discuss your answers in class. Have the page number available where you found the answer to help class discussion.

1. Explain why Thomas is excited about going to church that day.
2. Explain why Mr. and Mrs. Small are sitting on the hallway floor early Sunday morning.
3. Explain what two warnings Thomas thinks Mr. Pluto has left for them and what they mean.
4. Explain what plan Mr. Small has made up to help keep the family safe at night.
5. Explain how Mr. Pluto and Pesty are dressed and why that is so odd.
6. Explain why Mr. Small thought it was so odd that Mr. Pluto would say he was glad they had arrived and were feeling fine.
7. Explain what the platform is that Thomas stood on the previous night.
8. Explain what the AHHHH sound was that Thomas heard.

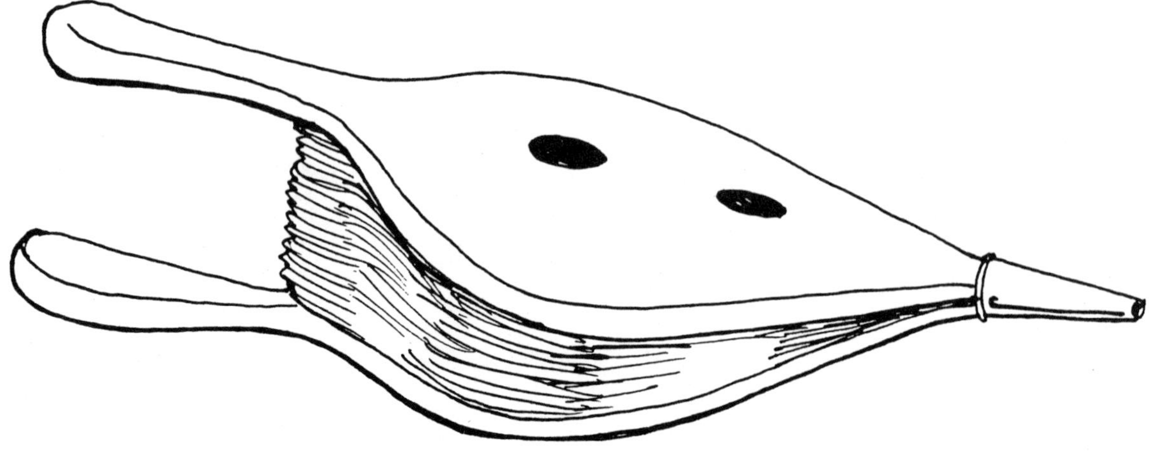

Name____ Date____________________

The House of Dies Drear

Productive Thinking

Three triangles all made of the same material and constructed in the same way:

- two legs made of wood
- the inside angle made of gold
- the surface made of metal painted silver
- a metal peg sticking out where the two wooden legs came together

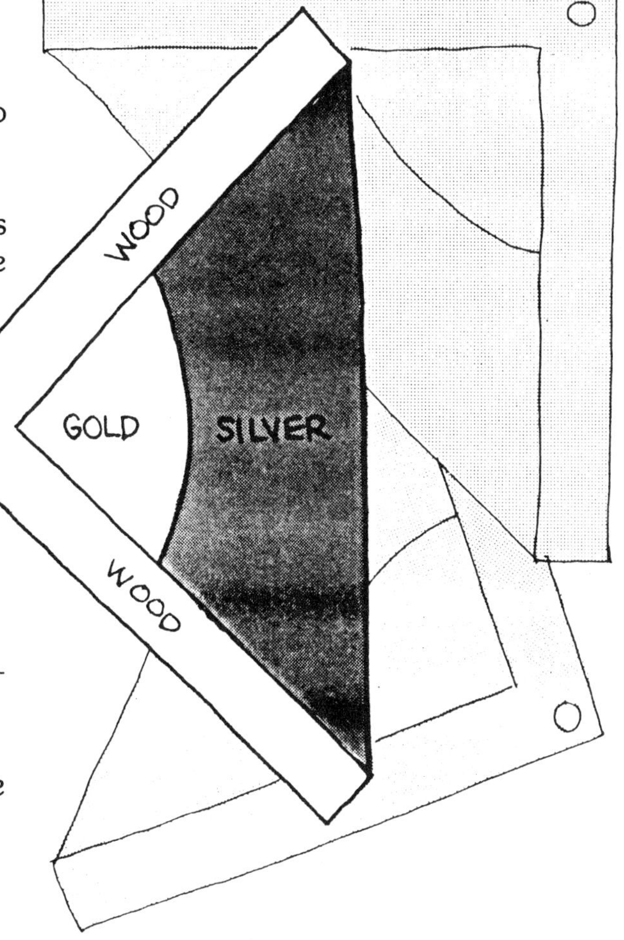

They all fit together perfectly, but one seems to be missing if you want to complete the cross they would form.

Is it meant to form a cross?

Is it meant to form a box?

Is it meant to be a warning?

Can they be fit together in any other way?

Does the color of the material mean anything?

Is there a piece missing, or could there be only three?

What does it mean?

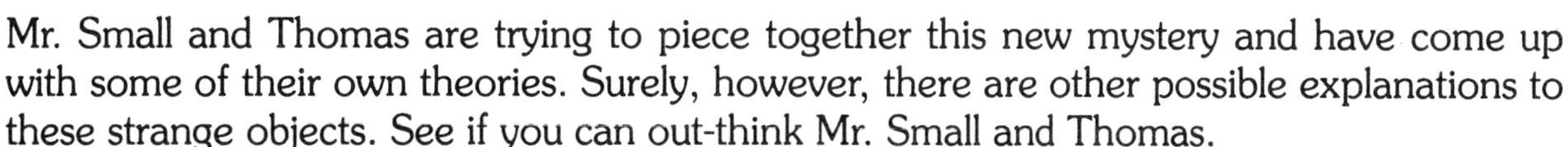

Mr. Small and Thomas are trying to piece together this new mystery and have come up with some of their own theories. Surely, however, there are other possible explanations to these strange objects. See if you can out-think Mr. Small and Thomas.

On your own paper use a little productive thinking to come up with many different and unusual possible explanations for what these objects could be.

To think productively you have to be willing to stretch your imagination in coming up with ideas. Use the Productive Thinking Guidelines sheet to help you out. Make a chart of your ideas and be ready to share them in class.

Productive Thinking Guidelines

Step One: Thinking Alone–How to Think Productively

Some of the world's best ideas began as dumb ideas. Who would ever have thought that by putting little scratches on a piece of metal that the entire recording industry would have started. Thomas Edison's friends may have even laughed out loud when he told them about his idea for the first time. What's the lesson? It's this: **No idea is a bad idea.**

To be a great productive thinker you have to be willing to record all ideas you come up with no matter how silly they seem at the moment. You will at first begin listing ideas that are most obvious. Then you'll get stumped and think there are no more ideas. That's when you've got to keep thinking and recording any and all ideas. No ideas are dumb. Don't evaluate any of the ideas and eliminate them. Just keep listing.

Another thing you've got to try to do is to think differently. People tend to get in thinking ruts. They think only one way. Approach the problem from a different angle. Keep asking, "What if...?"

On your own paper list as many different and unusual theories to what those three objects are as you can.

Step Two: Get a Partner and Think Together

The next step is to get together with a partner and share ideas. One of you will have to be recorder. The aim is to make a master list of ideas. This may not be as easy to do as it seems. You must follow two simple rules to make this work.

Rule 1: Reject no idea at all no matter how silly it may seem. Just make the list.

You will find that as you begin putting together this master list, an idea of your partner's will trigger an idea in you. It may be a completely new idea, or it may be a variation of his idea. The end result is more different and unusual ideas. The trick is not to laugh or throw out an idea just because it seems silly. You never know which idea will spark a better one.

Rule 2: Don't try to own your ideas.

Sometimes we think that an idea is terrific, and we don't want anyone fooling with it. That's not thinking productively. If you have an idea and your partner wants to add something to it, let him. His addition to your idea is just another new idea. Some people won't let anyone tamper with their ideas and want to argue the first time a suggestion is made. The only thing you do when you block a new idea is to stop creative thinking.

Name_______________________________________ Date____________________

Chapter 10: The House of Dies Drear

Before You Read

"Sit still and keep quiet." Have you ever heard those words before? The answer is probably, "Yes, many times." There are two worlds, the world of adults and the world of young children. The world of adults is a little slower at times, a little quieter at times. The world of young children is curiosity; it is moving and looking and asking and laughing.

In the adult world there are special times when sitting still and being quiet seems very important. These special times occur in church, at special ceremonies, in school, during meals on special days at home. You have probably had to suffer through some of those times when sitting still and keeping quiet were very important. Getting dressed up and staying clean sometimes goes along with these special times, too.

See if you can recall a time when, as a young child or even recently, you had to attend a ceremony or sit through a special occasion which required you to sit still and keep quiet. List that occasion below.

One time I had to sit still and keep quiet was ______________________________

____

Everyone knows how hard behaving in a proper and adult way can be for a young child. Kids squirm, move around, try to talk, think up excuses for getting up and do all sorts of things to survive the uncomfortableness of the situation. Can you recall how you handled the situation above?

On the lines below list some of the things you did during the time you were expected to sit still and keep quiet.

____

____

____

Now put these memories together into a story. Tell somebody about that time you had to sit still and be quiet. Include what the occasion was, whether you had to get dressed up, if you were given any warnings, what the setting was like, how you handled it, if you were able to sit still and if you weren't what happened.

If it will help, prepare for this storytelling by writing down some ideas on paper. Don't try to write it all out word for word. What you want to do is to *tell* the story, not read it.

Name______________________________ Date__________________

Chapter 10: The House of Dies Drear

As You Read

The entire story up to this point has focused on the Small family, the house and Mr. Pluto. In this chapter the story begins to open up. The Small family is going to go to church, a place where people are supposed to act in a certain, proper way. As you read notice first how Thomas feels about going to church, then how he feels once the service gets under way and finally how he feels when it is over.

In this chapter the Small family will also have a chance to meet some of the townspeople. Pay attention to how they react to this new family.

After You Read

Interpreting the Thoughts and Actions of Characters

Many strange things happened in this chapter. All of them have to do with what people said and how they behaved. Some of them have not been explained. That has been left for you to figure out. You will have to rely on what you know about the story and what you know about people in general in order to answer these questions. This kind of thinking is called interpreting.

Use your own paper to answer the questions below by interpreting the actions and thoughts of the different characters.

1. Early in this chapter, as the Small family enters the church, Thomas sees Mac Darrow and seems to have a kinder respect for him. The last time Thomas saw Mac Darrow he was angry with him. How do you interpret Thomas' change in attitude toward Mac Darrow?

2. Thomas thought that the townspeople will want to know what his father has to offer them and what he plans on taking away. Interpret what he means by this.

3. Thomas expected the townspeople to welcome his family. Instead the townspeople have a cold, almost hostile attitude toward them. Find two or three examples of their unfriendly behavior and then interpret why these townspeople are acting this way toward the Smalls.

4. The townspeople also seem angry that Mr. Pluto and Pesty have arrived for the church service. Find two examples that show their disapproval of Mr. Pluto and interpret why they feel this way.

5. During the ceremony Mr. Pluto behaves in a strange way. List some of the strange things he does and interpret why he acts this way.

Name____ Date____________________

Chapter 11: The House of Dies Drear

As You Read

Good readers of mysteries notice things. They notice important bits of information that don't seem important at the time but end up being important later. In this chapter some of that important information is presented to you, if you are wise enough to notice it.

As you read Chapter 11, find out what Mr. Small finds in his office. Then find out what Mr. Small and Thomas learn about Mr. Pluto and the Darrows.

After You Read

Memory Buster

How good were you at noticing important bits of information? You can test yourself by answering these questions. Try to answer them with the book closed. When you have answered as many as you can from memory, go back and check all your answers. Fill in any that you could not answer from memory. Then put the page number where you found the answer in the space following each question.

1. What did Thomas find in Mr. Small's office? p. _____

 ____

2. What does this thing that Thomas found match? p. _____

 ____

3. Why did Mr. Small go to the gas station owned by the Carrs? p. _____

 ____

4. List two things you learned about Mr. Pluto's background. p. _____

 ____

 ____

5. What strange things had the Darrows done on their land? p. _____

 ____

6. What warning does Mr. Carr give to Mr. Small? p. _____

 ____

Name____________________ Date__________

Chapter 11: The House of Dies Drear

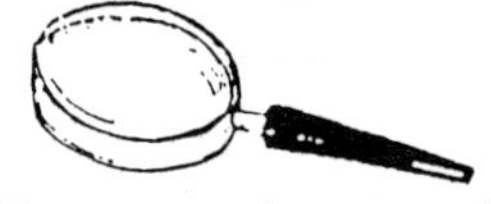

The Detective's Handbook

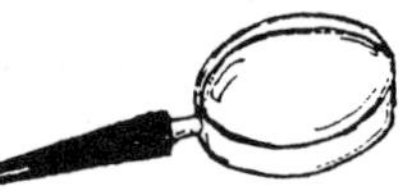

No crime has yet been committed, but peculiar things are happening, and they are happening with greater frequency. Perhaps it is time to make a record of all the strange events of this story. If you have been keeping a log of these events, now is the time to bring it out and look it over.

On the lines below list all the events of this story that seem to be extremely strange or even just a little peculiar to you. Fill in as many as you can. If you are really good at this and need more space, use your own paper to continue the list.

1. ____________________
2. ____________________
3. ____________________
4. ____________________
5. ____________________
6. ____________________
7. ____________________
8. ____________________
9. ____________________
10. ____________________

This list may seem confusing right now because you have listed many different and unusual events. Some of them are related and some are not. What you eventually want to do is find a pattern in what is happening. As you continue to read the story, look for more strange events and try to identify a pattern in them.

Name____ Date____________________

Chapter 11: The House of Dies Drear

As You Read

The Smalls continue to explore the town in this chapter before returning home. Unfortunately, things get nasty. Peculiar happenings become vicious. Read to find out what terrible thing happens.

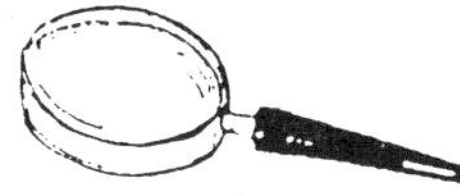

The Detective's Handbook

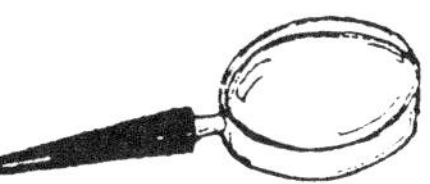

Who would do such a disgusting thing to the Small family? Even more importantly, why would they do it? Now is the time to sort out the information we have received so far in the story. What we want to learn is who has been harassing the Small family.

A detective will usually make out a chart of all the suspects when a crime has been committed. Below and on the following page is the outline of that chart. It is simple. It lists all the possible suspects in one column. After each one it leaves blocks to write in information about his motive (a motive is the reason why someone would want to commit the crime) and any important evidence or ideas related to that suspect. The more you are able to write about a suspect, the better able you will be to figure out a solution to the crime.

In developing your chart you will have to refer back to all chapters in the story. Perhaps some of those strange events and unexplained happenings will somehow begin to tie together now.

Suspect	Motive	Evidence/Ideas
1. Mr. Pluto		
2. The Darrows, including Mac and Pesty		

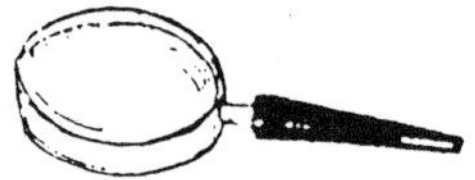

The Detective's Handbook

Suspect	Motive	Evidence/Ideas
3. The townspeople		
4. The ghost of Dies Drear		
5. Mr. Carr		
6. (other)		

On the lines below, write a short paragraph in which you explain who you think is guilty of this harassment. Did one person do it? Is it a conspiracy of many people? What is their motive? Be ready to share your ideas in class.

Name________________________________ Date____________________

Chapter 13: The House of Dies Drear

As You Read

You may think you know who is responsible for all that has been happening, but Mr. Small acts as if he is positive he knows. Read to find out where Mr. Small is headed. In this chapter the mystery just begins to unravel, if you read closely enough.

As you read this chapter make a note of any new information on your suspect chart.

Mr. Pluto's Cave

As Mr. Small and Thomas worked their way around the hill, they eventually came to another entrance to Mr. Pluto's cave. This is where he lives and so it is equipped with things a person would have in his house as well as some other interesting items. In the space below diagram Mr. Pluto's cave. Include as many of the following items as you can. By rereading parts of the chapter you will be able to visualize where everything is in the cave.

- the entrance tunnel
- the forge and bellows
- the brass bed
- the ladder
- the hanging rope
- the wall with harnesses, etc.
- the cooking stove and woodpile
- the tunnel leading to the horses
- the wall with photographs
- the carpeted area with armchair and table
- the wall with cooking utensils

35' wide

30' long

Name________________________________ Date________________

Chapter 14: The House of Dies Drear

Before You Read

Predicting

When Mr. Small pulled the rope the wall slid back, and what they saw was more than any dream or nightmare. What is it that they could have seen? On the lines below explain what it was they saw. You may want to consider some of the things Thomas saw when he went in the tunnel in Chapter 4, or you may want to reread the legend of Dies Drear from Chapter 2. One of them provides a clue.

When you are done describing your prediction, draw a sketch of it in the box below.

____

____

____

____

____

____

____

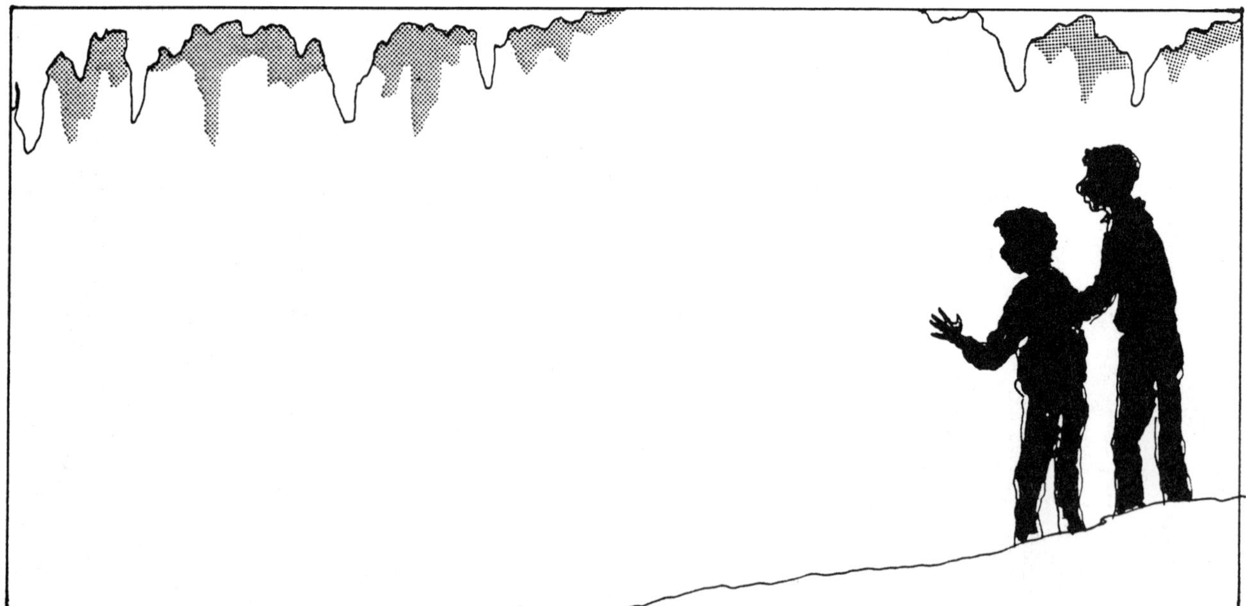

Now read to find out what Mr. Small and Thomas saw.

Name____________________________________ Date____________________

Chapter 14: The House of Dies Drear

After You Read

Details

Mr. Small and Thomas had come across the treasure of Dies Drear. This was not a treasure like you'd expect to find in a pirate's treasure chest nor was it mountains of gold. Carefully reread the section that describes Dies Drear's treasure and list as many items as you can on the lines below.

______________________________ ______________________________

______________________________ ______________________________

______________________________ ______________________________

______________________________ ______________________________

______________________________ ______________________________

______________________________ ______________________________

______________________________ ______________________________

______________________________ ______________________________

Name____ Date____________________

The House of Dies Drear

A Legacy

The word *legacy* has two definitions, a very specific one and a more general one. The more exact definition of a legacy is "money" or "property handed down through a will." Notice that money or property is specifically mentioned in this definition.

The more general definition is "anything handed down from an ancestor or predecessor or from the past." This definition is so much more general because first of all it says that a legacy can be anything. That would include real things like money or property as well as abstract things like a family history or a heritage. It is also general because it states that this legacy can be handed down by not only an ancestor but also by anyone who came before us. According to the second definition of *legacy* then, our freedom and the pride we Americans take in our freedom is a legacy handed down by the colonists, the early patriots and anyone else who fought for our freedom.

In this chapter Mr. Pluto talks a great deal about a legacy. He said that as boys he and River Swift Darrow (the Darrows' grandfather) searched the property of Dies Drear. River Swift searched for what he thought was his legacy. Mr. Pluto searched as well but for a different legacy.

Reread the part of the chapter in which that is discussed and on the lines below tell for what two different legacies each searched.

River Swift: ____

Mr. Pluto: ____

Your Own Legacy

It's hard to imagine, but someday you will be involved in legacies. Perhaps you are already. Take a moment to think what kind of legacy you want to leave your descendants. Either definition of *legacy* will do. On the lines below describe, as best you can and in any way you can, the legacy you would want to leave behind.

____

____

____

____

Name________________________________ Date______________

Chapter 15: The House of Dies Drear

As You Read

The knot that is this mystery continues to become untied in this chapter. Two Mr. Plutos? Vandalism? Devils? Cold stares by townspeople? Warnings? All of this is explained by just reading.

After You Read

Cause and Effect

Stacking dominoes can be an interesting hobby. The fun comes at the end when the first one is knocked down and all the rest fall one after the other. That is a perfect example of cause and effect.

In a story cause and effect are similar. One event happens and it causes something else to happen and so on. Use cause and effect thinking to complete each sentence below. Write what comes after the word *because*. The information comes from Chapters 14 and 15.

Example: The Small family moved into the house of Dies Drear *because*

Mr. Small leased the house when he got a job in the local college.

1. River Swift Darrow searched for treasure on the property of Dies Drear *because*

   ____

2. Mr. Pluto purposely developed a reputation as a devil *because*

   ____

3. The townspeople and the Darrows came to dislike Mr. Pluto *because*

   ____

4. Pluto's wife and son (Mayhew) left him years ago *because*

   ____

5. Mayhew returned and began impersonating his father *because*

   ____

6. Mr. Small grew suspicious that there were two Mr. Plutos *because*

   ____

7. The Darrows vandalized the Smalls' kitchen *because*

   ____

Name______________________________ Date________________

The House of Dies Drear

Similes

When writing a story, an author not only has to work out the plot and the characters and the setting, but he also has to develop the way the story is worded. In order to create believable characters, creative settings and a clearly imaginable plot, most writers will include figures of speech in their writing. There are many different figures of speech, but *The House of Dies Drear* develops several especially well.

A simile is a comparison between two things using the words *like* or *as*. For example, in Chapter 2 Mr. Small said that Mr. Pluto was agile *as* a cat. Mr. Pluto is being compared to a cat. In Chapter 5 the wings of birds are *like* pinwheels. Wings are compared to pinwheels. In both sentences the words *like* or *as* were used to make the comparison.

The House of Dies Drear uses similes to get the reader to visualize a scene or an object. Some of these similes are pointed out below. Finish them by looking them up in the chapter that is mentioned.

Chapter 13

1. What is Mr. Small's spirit like as he moves through the trees? ________________
2. What was Mr. Pluto's pacing like? ______________________________
3. What was Mr. Pluto's face like? ______________________________
4. What was the bellows in Mr. Pluto's cave compared to? ________________

Chapter 14

5. How did Pluto shake off Thomas? ______________________________
6. At the end of the chapter what did Mr. Pluto's voice sound like? ________________

Chapter 15

7. According to Mayhew, how do the Darrow boys act?________________________

Your Turn

Choose any scene in the story and develop your own similes to make that scene more imaginable.

Name________________________________ Date__________________

The House of Dies Drear

Planning

Before You Read

The Darrows have behaved very childishly, like boys who didn't grow up. By vandalizing the Smalls' kitchen, they hoped to scare the family out of the house. Now it's time for paybacks.

Mayhew seems to have a plan that will take care of the Darrows. It doesn't involve calling the police and having them locked up, and based on what we have learned about Mayhew and Mr. Pluto, it does not involve anything that will hurt them.

What is the plan?

Before reading about their plan, perhaps you could dream up a plan of your own. It couldn't be anything illegal like setting their house afire. It would have to be something that would make them look foolish or scare them.

Working alone or with someone else, devise a plan that will get back at the Darrows. Follow these steps in developing the plan on your own paper.

1. Decide on the outcome of the plan. What do you want the plan to accomplish?
2. Decide on the steps of the plan. List them in the order that they will occur.
3. Decide on any risks. List them and explain how they can be minimized.
4. List all the materials you will need.

Be prepared to share your plan in class.

Name________________________________ Date________________

Chapter 15: The House of Dies Drear

As You Read

Most, but not all of the mystery has been revealed. Now a plan is being hatched–a plan to get back at the mischief makers who vandalized the Smalls' house and who have threatened Mr. Pluto most of his life. Read to find out what the plan might be. It is not fully explained, but by reading closely you'll get enough clues to figure out most of it.

After You Read

Memory Buster

Have you figured out the plan yet? Answer the questions below to sort out all the information you received in this chapter. Do this with the book closed. When you are done, check your answers by putting the page number where you found the answer in the space after the question.

1. What talent does Mayhew have that he will use in his plan? p. _____

    ____

2. Where will Mr. Pluto be when they are carrying out the plan? p. _____

    ____

3. Why is it necessary to let everyone know that Mr. Pluto is gone? p. _____

    ____

4. Where do the Smalls have to go to get supplies? p. _____

    ____

5. What will Mr. Small be wearing, and how will Thomas and Mrs. Small be dressed? p. _____

    ____

Based on all this information, explain what you think their plan is. Do this on your own paper and be ready to share it in class.

Name______________________________ Date________________

Chapter 17: The House of Dies Drear

As You Read

Not all the mystery has been unraveled yet, but it will now. There still have been unanswered questions.

1. What is the meaning of those triangles?
2. Why has Mr. Pluto been so intense on protecting this property for all these years as only a groundskeeper?
3. If Dies Drear came from the East with a Mohegan, what ever happened to that Mohegan?
4. Finally (if we go all the way back to Chapter 2), whatever became of the third slave in the legend?

These are the questions on which to focus your attention as you read Chapter 17.

After You Read

On the lines below answer the above questions. Write in complete sentences and use more than one sentence if necessary.

1. ______________________________

2. ______________________________

3. ______________________________

4. ______________________________

Name________________________________ Date________________

The House of Dies Drear

Map Reading

Dies Drear had a way of steering the runaway slaves through the land that separated them from freedom. Each slave who knew the system could weave his way to safety without an escort. That system involved the triangles that Mr. Small found in his home and office. Each triangle, when positioned a certain way, told the person which way to go.

In order to complete the map reading activity below, you will need to know the direction each triangle signifies. Reread that part of Chapter 17 in order to clearly understand the system.

Can You Find Your Way?

Below is a map of a forest. Each tree has a letter assigned to it and a triangle on it. Beginning with the tree marked *A*, follow the triangles from tree to tree until you reach the safety of the church. The object of this activity is to follow the correct path. When you are done, list the trees by letter in the order you followed. Compare your route to that of others. The correct route will be given later.

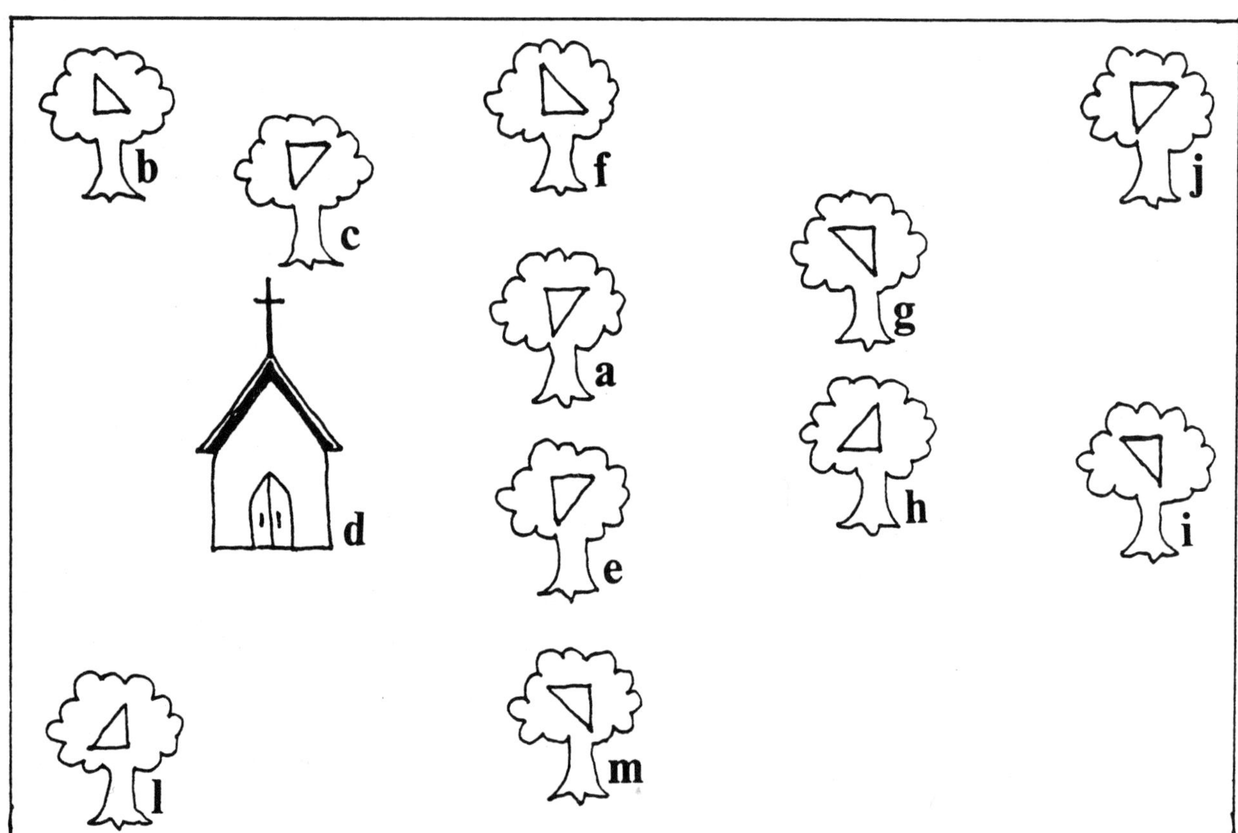

The route I followed was:

1. _____ 3. _____ 5. _____ 7. _____ 9. _____ 11. _____

2. _____ 4. _____ 6. _____ 8. _____ 10. _____ 12. _____

Name______________________________ Date______________

Chapter 18: The House of Dies Drear

Before You Read

There have been a lot of characters in this story. Some of them were pretty strange...at least at first...while some were plain. A few were cruel and some were friendly. Several of them are quite forgettable, but others are memorable. Of all the memorable ones, certainly Mr. Pluto and his son Mayhew would have to be counted. Both men seemed larger than life itself. They were almost unreal. That is why it seems odd that Thomas came to trust Mayhew and Mr. Pluto so quickly.

At the end of Chapter 17 it says that Thomas knew that frightening the Darrows was going to be scary. Still, he trusted Mayhew enough to go ahead with the plan even though he did not know what that plan involved. Mr. Small seems to trust Mayhew just as much because he is willing to get his family involved in this plan. So what is it about Mayhew that is so trustworthy?

Perhaps you have known people that you could trust right from the start. Take a moment to recall people like that as well as people that you learned to trust over time. On the lines below list the names of those people. Make sure you list only those people you find trustworthy, not just your friends. You may include people you don't know too well because you feel they are trustworthy.

______________________ ______________________

______________________ ______________________

______________________ ______________________

Now look over the list of people and try to figure out what it is that makes these people so trustworthy. On the lines below list the "ingredients" for the making of a trustworthy person. Be ready to discuss your idea in class.

Ingredients for Trustworthiness

______________________ ______________________

______________________ ______________________

______________________ ______________________

As You Read

It's time to finish the book. Read Chapter 18 to find out what the plan is that will scare the Darrows and whether it works. Notice at the end of the chapter how Mayhew treats Thomas. That should give a clue as to why Thomas feels he can trust him.

Name______________________________ Date________________

The House of Dies Drear

Sequencing

A lot has happened in this story. Many separate episodes taken together form a mystery. See if you can remember the order in which each episode happened with your book closed. In the first set of spaces put a 1 in front of the event that happened first, a 2 in front of the event that happened second and so on. When you are done, check the book to see if you are correct, and use the second set of spaces to make any corrections. There are twelve events listed.

_____ _____ Mr. Small and Thomas learn that Mayhew Skinner has been impersonating his father, Mr. Pluto.

_____ _____ Thomas falls into one of the tunnels and is terrified by a strange sound.

_____ _____ Mayhew, the Smalls and Mr. Pluto carry out a plan to scare and humiliate the Darrows so that they will leave everyone alone.

_____ _____ Three triangles are placed in the house at night to scare the Small family.

_____ _____ Mr. Small learns about the Darrow family from Mr. Carr.

_____ _____ Thomas learns of the legend of Dies Drear and the house they are going to move into.

_____ _____ The Small family returns home to find their home vandalized.

_____ _____ Thomas is frightened by Mr. Pluto when he is led to Mr. Pluto's cave by a strange sound.

_____ _____ While trying to find Mr. Pluto, Mr. Small and Thomas stumble upon the treasure of Dies Drear hidden deep in a cave.

_____ _____ Thomas enters the house and decides that he dislikes Mr. Pluto despite the fact that he has never met him.

_____ _____ Mr. Small learns that it was the Darrows that vandalized his home in order to scare them out of the house.

_____ _____ The Small family get a very cold reception at church.

A Complete Summary

Using the sentences above as a guide, write a paragraph of the events of this story. You will not be able to just copy each sentence in order. You will need to change the wording and add connecting words like *next* or *after*. If you want to add events not mentioned, that is fine, too.

Name____ Date____________________

Chapter 19: The House of Dies Drear

As You Read

All the action of the story seems to be over, but there are still some loose ends that need to be tied up in this mystery. Read to find out what will become of Mr. Pluto, what will happen to the treasure of Dies Drear, if Mac and Thomas will ever be able to get together as friends and why the Darrows will probably not try to get back at everyone.

After You Read

Tying Up Loose Ends

On the lines below answer each question. Be ready to share your answers and show where in the chapter you found them.

1. What decision has Mr. Small made about dealing with the secret treasure of Dies Drear?

____

____

2. What will become of Mr. Pluto now that he no longer has to protect the legend and the treasure?

____

____

3. Why can the Smalls and Mr. Pluto feel safe that the Darrows will leave them alone?

____

____

4. Can Mac Darrow and Thomas ever be friends since Thomas played a part in humiliating his family?

____

____

Supplemental Vocabulary

Not all lessons contain vocabulary work. Nonetheless, you may want to supplement your teaching with additional vocabulary work from time to time. Below are additional lists of words by chapters. No more than seven words per chapter are included. Chapters 2, 3, 6 and 7 are excluded since those chapters already have vocabulary lessons.

Chapter 1

1. craven
2. chicory
3. foothills
4. sinister
5. rise
6. sprawling
7. whittle

Chapter 4

1. serene
2. foundation
3. notion
4. forlorn
5. impact
6. hewn

Chapter 5

1. brackish
2. gaping
3. varicolored
4. loomed
5. crestfallen
6. tamper
7. meander

Chapter 8

1. superstitious
2. cubicles
3. hearth
4. cumbersome
5. mantel
6. ornate
7. parlor

Chapter 9

1. minister
2. hypotenuse
3. intruders
4. confide
5. fondly
6. bellows
7. sheepishly

Chapter 10

1. vestibule
2. pew
3. feigned
4. clannish
5. hymnals
6. congregation
7. bemused

Chapter 11

1. skeleton key
2. jimmy
3. prejudiced
4. vandalism
5. rednecks

Chapter12

1. tread
2. devilment
3. frigidaire
4. evaporated milk

Chapter 13

1. outcropping
2. sconces
3. scoundrels
4. forge

Chapter 14

1. tapestries
2. eccentric
3. interspersed
4. embroidered
5. curator
6. ledgers
7. phantasm

Chapter 15

1. obsessed
2. fanatical
3. heritage
4. belittle
5. zeal
6. venture

Chapter 16

1. anguish
2. hypodermic
3. pensively
4. reprimand
5. peeved
6. family
7. rascals

Chapter 17

1. shroud
2. squatter
3. premonition
4. inkling
5. dank
6. fare
7. steadfastness

Chapter 18

1. phosphorous
2. subtle
3. apparition
4. grotesque
5. gossamer
6. withers
7. specter

Chapter 19

1. intricate
2. mistily
3. inquire

Extension Activities

Historical Reporting

The reading of this book naturally leads students to all sorts of investigations. By just hooking onto the idea of African American culture throughout our country's history, many possible topics can be developed including those directly related to the underground railroad such as

- the running of the underground railroad
- famous conductors of the underground railroad including Levi Coffin, William Still and Harriet Tubman
- Fugitive Slave Laws: what were they and how were they enforced
- famous abolitionists
- The underground railroad in Ohio (The book entitled *The Mysteries of Ohio's Underground Railroad* by Wilbur Henry Siebert provides a wealth of information as does another of his books entitled *The Underground Railroad from Slavery to Freedom* which includes maps of underground railroad routes.)
- methods of escape
- the use of segregated churches in the underground railroad

and those related to African American culture and history in general including

- African American spiritual hymns
- black slave culture of the U.S. prior to the Civil War
- segregation practices in the U.S. after the Civil War
- the Civil Rights Act of 1964
- the role of Martin Luther King, Jr., in promoting civil rights in the U.S.
- African American leaders of your community

The Trunk

At the end of the story Thomas notices a trunk suspended from the ceiling of the cave, and he immediately wonders what could be in it. Students can employ the Productive Thinking Guidelines on page 140 to work together in order to come up with many, different and unusual items that the trunk could hold.

After a list of possible items are developed, students can individually select those items they think are most likely to be in the trunk and discuss why they think so. Remember that the items cannot be so large that they wouldn't fit nor so heavy that they could not be hoisted and held by a rope for many years.

Character Portraits

Early in the reading of the book, tell students that they are to begin looking through magazines and books for pictures of people. Their task is to find pictures of people that look like what they imagine the characters of the story look like. They can cut these pictures out or photocopy them. Each is then to create a photojournal of all the characters.

Collections

Dies Drear collected many things for no other reason than because they seemed collectible. Have students share their collections in class. They can not only bring them in intermittently and display them, but also prepare short presentations in which they tell about their collections. Plan on a lot of baseball and basketball card collections as well as doll and stuffed animal collections.

Variation

Begin a classroom collection. Students contribute to a collection of items that becomes the "Official Room ___ Collection of ____." Some interesting items can include rocks, stamps, stickers, pieces of cloth, sugar packets from restaurants, leaves, signatures, bumper sticker sayings, advertising slogans, pencils, etc. This collection can end with the school year or become a permanent fixture in the room.

Variation

Have each student fill a box with items that he feels are perfect representations of himself. These are items that reflect the student's life-style, culture, history, etc. The box can be decorated, filled and then brought in to share. A display of these boxes can be made and labeled as artifacts of that student's life.

To make a game out of it, students can bring in their boxes unlabeled, and they can be set up around the room. Students can then look at them trying to match each box to the student.

You may even label the box "A Legacy Box" and tell students to include items of theirs that they would want to pass on to other members of their families or friends.

Name the Chapters

None of the chapters have names. Working in pairs or individually, students can come up with appropriate titles for each chapter or a set of chapters. All the chapter names can be presented in class with a vote for the best name for each chapter. A chart of the chapter names can then be made and displayed.

Variation

Create title pages complete with name and number of the chapter along with an illustration of an interesting scene from that chapter. These, too, can be mounted and displayed around the room.

Rewrite an Episode: Creative Writing

A mystery story always reaches a point where the plot could go in several different directions. Working as a group or in pairs, have students identify those episodes and loosely discuss alternative directions for the plot. After a class sharing of these ideas, have students rewrite one of the episodes making the suggested change. Have them look closely at the author's style as well as the character development so that they can accurately rewrite that part of the story. A reading of these alternatives can be made in class.

Answer Key

Setting Page 4
1. present
2. at home
3. Chateau Bow-Wow
4. (interpretive)

Characters Page 5
1. Harold
2. Chester
3. Toby, Pete, Mr. and Mrs. Monroe

Plot Page 6
1. leaving pets behind
2. eating
3. he hates it
4. food, strangers, the place is for dogs
5. tries to hide
6. There's trouble ahead.

Base Words Page 8

1. fit	8. assure
2. fate	9. sound
3. content	10. fiend
4. sense	11. impress
5. easy	12. back
6. carry	13. sullen
7. sensitive	14. dry

1. restless and full of tension
2. a box used to carry an animal
3. in an evil sort of way
4. to make a long, repeating sound
5. to say something in a dry, sarcastic way

Descriptive Page 11

1. D	5. B
2. E	6. C
3. G	7. A
4. F	

Memory Buster Page 12
1. raining
2. works hard then doesn't
3. exercise
4. job
5. a murder
6. thinks he's flirting
7. He doesn't scare her.

STQ–go around the outside wall

Cause and Effect Page 14
1. Dr. Greenbriar is going on vacation
2. they are flirting
3. she yells at him
4. they howl at night
5. clumsy

Context Clues Page 19
1. feeling worried or tense
2. to answer back
3. a pitiful look
4. in deep thought
5. working together with someone
6. not as strong
7. to listen secretly to others
8. to stare at someone angrily
9. to bother or disturb

Sequencing Page 21
6, 3, 10, 2, 7, 1, 8, 4, 9, 5

Memory Buster Page 29
1. Heather and Howard
2. Taxi
3. Max and Georgette
4. Taxi, Harold, Lyle
5. howling
6. Chester
7. Chester

Fact or Opinion Page 30

1. O	6. F
2. F	7. O
3. O	8. O
4. O	9. O
5. F	10. F

Vocabulary Page 31
1. in a frightening way
2. a confused look
3. to move quietly
4. to question
5. something thrown away
6. to make bigger or louder
7. with lots of expression

Cause and Effect Page 32
1. they needed help
2. they needed to find Heather and Howard
3. they were ready to have pups
4. he wanted to save Heather and Howard
5. he was told to
6. Harrison answered the phone, and the dogs were barking outside his house.
7. he wanted money

After You Read Page 34
1. trying to find the valuable one for ransom
2. In both cases he was able to blame Jill.
3. Harrison told him
4. looked in files
5. looking for Louise; Taxi
6. no
7. nervous over upcoming births

Setting Page 42
1. present
2. September
3. city
4. professor's store
5. professor is so quiet and strange

Characters Page 43
April, Caroline, Dorothea, Professor

Plot
1. back of his store getting something
2. loose board
3. bust of Nefertiti
4. curtain and dirty window

April Page 45
1. sent by mother until she's not touring so much
2. "only a little while"
3. (interpretive)
4. rude behavior
5. (interpretive)
6. likes old stuff
7. her name and where she's from

Caroline Page 45
1. grandmother
2. to avoid an argument
3. moved to allow her to have a room of her own

The Professor Page 46
1. old artifacts
2. talks little, etc.
3. shows no emotion

Dorothea
1. mother
2. daughter-in-law
3. vocalist
4. died in Korea
5. not be bothered

Melanie
1. eleven
2. greeter
3. (interpretive)
4. imaginative

Marshall
1. (interpretive)
2. a stuffed octopus; security

Base Words Page 47

1. sympathy	6. comfort
2. accumulate	7. donate
3. impress	8. wary
4. trim	9. defy
5. casual	10. sober

Memory Buster Page 51
1. She admired the game.
2. Mrs. Ross calling them
3. A girl was killed.
4. the professor
5. windows broken
6. made costumes
7. continues to tour

Cause and Effect Page 55
1. it was arranged they have lunch
2. they found the bust of Nefertiti in the storage yard
3. loose board
4. a girl was killed
5. they plotted to sneak away during Halloween

Context Clues Page 57
B, A, A, B, B, A, B, A

Sequencing Page 58
9, 4, 1, 5, 7, 6, 10, 8, 2, 3

Moods and Maybes Pages 60-61
1. broke costume
2. Mr. Ross
3. Nick; no room
4. Toby

STQ–in the hollow base of the statue of Diana

5. Set
6. (many answers)
7. finish alphabet
8. Elizabeth–Nefertiti; Marshall–Marshamosis; April–Bastet; Ken–Horemheb; Melanie–Aida; Toby–Ramose
9. his cousin
10. how to write hieroglyphics
11. had a job

STQ–the window

Step-by-Step Page 65

1 procession	5. clean bird
3. prepare brine	7. wrap bird
4. soak in brine	8. bury bird

Memory Buster Page 67

1. school	7. Ken
2. prophecy	8. April
3. April	9. It was answered.
4. Toby's	10. (See book.)
5. owl	11. try again
6. written	STQ (See book.)

Ceremony for Answering... Page 68

2. procession	7. three hairs in fire
3. April to altar	8. chanting
5. April bows low	9. April stops chanting
6. walk and sprinkle holy water	10. read oracle

Fact or Opinion Page 72

1. O
2. F
3. O
4. F
5. F
6. O
7. O
8. F
9. F
10. O

Cause and Effect Page 74

1. wanted to play
2. it was in code
3. parakeet died
4. wanted to see paper
5. he didn't know the answer
6. forgot math book
7. he'd seen him watching before
8. he suspected cousin

Setting Page 83

1. 1951
2. winter
3. Massachusetts
4. grandparents' home

Characters Page 84

1. Johnny, Grandpa, Gramma, Professor
2. Father Baart, Nemo, Johnny's father, Johnny's mother, Mr. Herman, Mrs. Mumaw

Plot Page 85

1. mother dead; father in Korea
2. got car out of snow
3. ancient Egypt
4. Nemo
5. Mrs. Mumaw was run over by horses. Mr. Herman was crushed by stone.
6. disappeared

Vocabulary Page 87

B, B, A, B, A, A, A, B, A, B

Memory Buster Pages 94-95

1. scared by a sound
2. fussing
3. was a hoax; the sticker on the bottom
4. as burial objects
5. keep it and write to learn more
6. a man

STQ–Middle Ages

Clues Page 95

3. M
4. M
5. S
6. S
7. S
8. M
9. M
10. M

Cause and Effect Page 98

1. spiders infested the house
2. he still thinks the curse is real
3. of his worry
4. helping with paper drive
5. she asked for her watch
6. he was going to steal the watch
7. (interpretive)
8. he curses Eddie

Memory Buster Page 100

1. broke his arm
2. his curse
3. see professor
4. Mr. Beard
5. pretend to use the power of the figurine to make him strong
6. been in his family
7. not guilty; good spirits

STQ–lit candles

Sequencing Page 101

7, 3, 10, 6, 1, 9, 4, 5, 2, 8

Base Words Page 103

1. swivel
2. figure
3. grumble
4. mood
5. accuse
6. triumph
7. resist
8. bed
9. process
10. terror
11. accuse
12. amuse
13. tone

Fact or Opinion Page 104

1. F
2. O
3. O
4. O
5. F
6. F
7. O
8. F

Sequencing Page 108

10, 2, 11, 8, 1, 4, 3, 7, 5, 9, 6

Similes Page 110

1. the plague
2. a windup toy soldier
3. if it were on fire
4. a dynamite bomb
5. a dark cloud on the horizon
6. church mice

Memory Buster Page 114

1. New Hampshire
2. never seen them
3. a rock formation
4. cigarettes
5. an underlined passage in the Bible
6. Father Baart
7. put on the ring and leave

Cause and Effect Page 116

1. he does not know Dutch or German
2. of the footprints in mud
3. it went to Angel's Scenic View as mentioned in Father Baart's last message
4. he has a flashlight
5. the professor removes the ring
6. the ashes of Father Baart are there
7. the fire goes out

Setting Page 125

1. in a car
2. North Carolina
3. Ohio
4. (Answers may vary.)

Characters

1. not in favor of it
2. professor; college graduate
3. 13; whittling
4. The chapter focuses on his experiences.
5. cry easily; Thomas can hold them both

Plot

1. (Refer to book.)
2. not to go to the house
3. (Refer to book.)

Mystery Unfolds Page 127

F, M, M, F, M, M, M, F, F, M, M, F

Sequencing Page 131

7, 5, 1, 10, 6, 3, 8, 4, 9, 2

Vocabulary Page 134

1. the young buds of a plant
2. to nap lightly
3. the cheeks
4. a general impression or feeling
5. a piece of wood placed beneath a door
6. pleasant and sincere
7. crafty in appearance
8. completely or totally
9. a reddish-brown horse
10. to tie an animal's feet in order to restrain it

Memory Buster Page 137

1. wore gloves
2. coffee
3. It's Sunday.
4. far from the stairs
5. chair facing away from bed
6. in the parlor
7. through secret door
8. place an object by each bedroom door

Explain It Page 138

1. he'll meet people; show off his whittling
2. looking at triangles
3. arrangement of parlor; the triangles
4. Mr. Small and Thomas stay up in shifts to guard.
5. dressed as one would 100 years ago
6. Mr. Pluto had greeted them yesterday.
7. roof of Mr. Pluto's cave
8. bellows

Memory Buster Page 143

1. a triangle
2. the other triangles
3. to enquire about getting a lock fixed
4. Mr. Pluto came from somewhere else as a boy; bad blood between Pluto and Darrows
5. dug up trees and even moved house to look under
6. watch out for the Darrows

Details Page 149

French Renaissance desk, tapestries, shoes, totem poles, jewelry, chains of gold, silks, wood chests, glassware, ledgers, canoes, embroidered material

Cause and Effect Page 151

1. he believed the treasure was his legacy
2. he wanted to scare people
3. they saw him as strange
4. hated people's attitude toward them
5. his dad was sick
6. Mayhew wore a glove; he mentioned India
7. they wanted to scare the Smalls out

Similes Page 152

1. like a handprint
2. like a flacon
3. like a bearded pirate
4. an old man
5. like a lion shaking off ticks
6. a hundred rushing voices
7. like vandals on Halloween

Memory Buster Page 154

1. acting
2. in hospital
3. to entice Darrows
4. a Columbus theater shop
5. a black suit; as slaves

Map Reading Page 156

A, E, M, L, B, F, J, I, H, G, C, D

Sequencing Page 158

10, 3, 12, 5, 6, 1, 8, 4, 9, 2, 11, 7